WALK ▸ JOG ▸ RUN

A Free-Motion Quilting Workout

MUSCLE-MEMORY-BUILDING EXERCISES,
PROJECTS & TIPS

Dara Tomasson

an imprint of C&T Publishing

Text copyright © 2020 by Dara Tomasson
Photography and artwork copyright © 2020 by C&T Publishing, Inc.

Publisher: Amy Barrett-Daffin
Creative Director: Gailen Runge
Acquisitions Editor: Roxane Cerda
Managing Editor: Liz Aneloski
Editor: Beth Baumgartel
Technical Editor: Julie Waldman
Cover/Book Designer: April Mostek
Production Coordinator: Zinnia Heinzmann
Production Editor: Alice Mace Nakanishi
Illustrator: Valyrie Gillum
Photo Assistants: Rachel Holmes and Gregory Ligman
Cover photography by Estefany Gonzalez of C&T Publishing, Inc.
Lifestyle and instructional photography by Vanessa Lust Photography, unless otherwise noted; subjects photography by Kelly Burgoyne, Estefany Gonzalez, and Diane Pedersen of C&T Publishing, Inc., unless otherwise noted

Published by Stash Books, an imprint of C&T Publishing, Inc., P.O. Box 1456, Lafayette, CA 94549

Library of Congress Cataloging-in-Publication Data
Names: Tomasson, Dara, 1973- author.
Title: Walk, jog, run-a free-motion quilting workout : muscle-memory-building exercises, projects & tips / Dara Tomasson.
Description: Lafayette, CA : Stash Books, 2020.
Identifiers: LCCN 2019049047 | ISBN 9781617459153 (trade paperback) | ISBN 9781617459160 (ebook)
Subjects: LCSH: Machine quilting--Patterns.
Classification: LCC TT835 .T643 2020 | DDC 746.46/041--dc23
LC record available at https://lccn.loc.gov/2019049047

Printed in the USA
10 9 8 7 6 5 4 3 2 1

Dedication

To Grandmas Mary and Hazel, for their legacy of creating beauty with their hands and teaching the importance of community by surrounding themselves with other women. I strive to follow your examples as I continue to educate, inspire others, and build both physical and digital communities.

To my incredible children, who cheer me on.

To my husband, who is by far my greatest supporter. He realizes that a wife who can create with quilts and then teach those skills to others, shares her personal joy, which in turn equals more joy in our home.

Acknowledgments

I am grateful to the following people and companies:

- Cindy Cloward of Riley Blake Designs who believes in me and my skills. Your generosity in providing the fabric for this book is heartwarming. Producing beautiful fabric to inspire these projects and create more beauty in our lives is truly meaningful work!

- Superior Threads for designing the perfect thread for my machine. I appreciate their support.

- Gammill and Brother sewing machine manufacturers for producing amazing machines that allow me to play, create, and make quilts that bring so much love and joy to so many.

- Stephanie Hackney and Hobbs Bonded Fibers Company for jumping on board to support this book.

- C&T Publishing for this opportunity to share my skills and knowledge.

- Nikki Clarke Murray at Stacked Fabrics for her incredible eye coordinating the amazing fabric combinations for my patterns. Her generosity of time and talents is truly remarkable. She went over and above what I originally asked her to do.

- All the pattern testers who so generously gave of their time and provided such valuable feedback: Jamie Manning, Becky Keizer, Angela Purrenhage, Tara Sinclair, Nilufer Algas, Carol Shaw, Sarah Miller, Ainhoa Castellanos, Charlotte Burns, Sheila Hooper, Emily Beth Walton, Moira Porter, and Arlene Veenhof.

- Julia Wentzell whose support was so needed and appreciated.

- The friends who brought me twenty pizzas at a time.

CONTENTS

Introduction 6

SECTION I:
FOUNDATION BUILDING 9

**Chapter 1: Sewing Machines and
Other Supplies 10**

Sewing Machines 10

Needles and Bobbins 13

Presser Feet 15

Drawing Implements and Writing Surfaces 17

Understanding Sewing Machine Tension 20

Maintenance 21

**Chapter 2: Thread, Fabric,
and Batting 22**

**Chapter 3: Setting up Your Sewing
Space and Setting Goals 28**

Chapter 4: Basic Skills 32

Basics of Free-Motion Quilting 32

Making a Quilt Sandwich 33

Basting a Quilt 34

Making and Attaching Binding 37

Quilt Labels: A Special Touch 39

Foundation Building Practice Workouts 40

SECTION II:
DESIGN ELEMENTS AND PROJECTS   41

Chapter 5: Straight-Line Quilting   42

Design Element: Straight Lines

PROJECT: On a Roll
Pencil Holder   46

Chapter 6: Quilting Directional e's and l's   50

Design Elements: e's and l's

PROJECT: Tote–ally Terrific
Tote Bag   54

Chapter 7: Quilting Loops   60

Design Element: Loops

PROJECT: Heart of the Home
Pillow Cover   64

Chapter 8: Quilting Daisies   70

Design Element: Daisies

PROJECT: He Loves Me,
He Loves Me Not Apron   74

Chapter 9: Quilting Paisleys   82

Design Element: Paisleys

PROJECT: Ohio Star
Table Runner   86

Chapter 10: Quilting Stipple, Meandering, and Puzzle Designs   92

Design Elements: Stippling, Meandering, and Puzzles

PROJECT: So Happy Together
Place Mats   96

Chapter 11: Quilting Circuit Boards   102

Design Element: Circuit Boards

PROJECT: Technically Speaking
Computer Sleeve   106

Chapter 12: Quilting Wishbones and Fancy L's   112

Design Elements: Wishbones and Fancy L's

PROJECT: Continuous Fancy Eights
Builder Quilt   116

Chapter 13: Quilting Ribbon Candy   120

Design Element: Ribbon Candy Curves

PROJECT: X's and O's Quilt   124

Chapter 14: Quilting Clamshells   130

Design Element: Clamshells

PROJECT: Checkerboard Quilt Set   134

Appendix   139

BONUS! Sawtooth Star Block   139

Resources   140

About the Author   143

54

74

96

116

134

INTRODUCTION

Think of free-motion quilting (FMQ) as doodling on fabric with thread!

This book is a beginner's guide to free-motion quilting, with basic foundational information, skill development, stitching tips, design options, and project ideas for a successful start in the process of free-motion quilting.

Traditionally, quilters tend to stitch in straight lines with a standard presser foot or a walking foot. And, while I am a fan of straight-line quilting, I never wanted to be restricted to quilting only with straight lines. I started my quilting journey in the early 90s with a twin-size quilt that took me a very long time to hand quilt. I had no clue that there was a way to quilt it on my sewing machine! This lead me to creative exploration of free-motion quilting, which has brought my joy of creating and quilting to a whole new level.

I call myself "free-motion quilting liberator" because I added a whole new layer of creativity to my finished projects. Don't be afraid to quilt beyond the lines! With this book, I share with you everything I learned through trial and error; how to choose the correct thread and batting; learning the importance of thread tension; basting the layers; and stitching beyond the lines! I have helped quilters overcome the challenges inherent in free-motion quilting in my classes, both in person and online, through my blog, and now, much to my delight, in this book.

HOW TO USE THIS BOOK

If you are just beginning to explore free-motion quilting or you feel stuck in your free-motion quilting journey, I recommend that you make a conscious decision to learn and expand your creative potential through setting up goals and using the workout exercises to commit and learn this fabulous art form.

In each of the **Section II chapters**, there is a *specific design element* for you to learn, with step-by-step instructions, to help you build a solid foundation of free-motion quilting skills; *workout exercises* to help develop and practice your new skills; and a *project* to showcase your talents.

I have had the privilege of teaching hundreds of students this tried-and-true method of learning free-motion quilting.

- The free-motion designs are divided into basic elements, making the entire design easier to stitch. It is so fun to watch my students learn that through tweaking or changing a small element of the design, they can create new designs.

- The ten practice workouts help you build your skills and endurance. The workouts are meant to provide encouragement and training. Make a goal, break it down, commit to it, evaluate your progress, reevaluate, and continue to progress. Scheduling pockets of time for these workouts is crucial for developing muscle memory.

- The projects will help satisfy your desire to create new and beautiful quilted items.

Walk, Jog, and Run to Free-Motion Quilting Success

What goals do you have for free-motion quilting? The workouts and projects in the following chapters will take you from walking to jogging to running, through a wonderful meandering journey of free-motion quilting.

WALK

SIMPLE FREE-MOTION QUILTER

- You have proficient knowledge of quilting supplies (sewing machine, thread, needles, and so on).

- You are comfortable using a walking foot to produce several designs.

- You can use the darning foot to produce e's and l's and other linear designs.

JOG

MODERATE FREE-MOTION QUILTER

- You know how to divide a quilt for an all over design.

- You can stitch loops, daisies, paisleys, stipple stitches, and circuit board designs.

RUN

ACCOMPLISHED FREE-MOTION QUILTER

- You are confident creating wishbone, ribbon candy, and clamshell designs, as well as many variations of all the designs featured in the project.

SECTION I

FOUNDATION BUILDING

These chapters contain information on the foundation for successful free-motion quilting! Take the time to practice the workouts at the end this section; you'll be surprised how helpful it is to build muscle memory for free-motion quilting and stitching beyond straight lines.

CHAPTER 1

Sewing Machines and Other Supplies

The right sewing machine, tools, supplies, threads, and notions make it easier to learn about and enjoy the skill of free-motion stitching. A better understanding of some parts and features, as well as the mechanics of sewing machines, will empower you to really understand and appreciate your machine and use it to its fullest potential. As you experiment with new stitches demonstrated throughout this book, you can use this chapter as a reference.

SEWING MACHINES

You don't need a state-of-the-art sewing machine to free-motion quilt, but there are a few features that will make your free-motion stitching easier and more professional looking. Here are several that I find extremely helpful, which probably means you will appreciate them too. Knowledge is power!

▶ **DARA'S TIP** *If you are considering purchasing a new sewing machine, I'll share the advice I give to all my students: "Do your research, test a variety of machines using a variety of fabric swatches, talk to fellow quilters, spend time at a reputable dealership, and buy from a dealership rather than a big box store; a relationship with your sewing machine retailer is so valuable."*

Power and Speed

For free-motion quilting, I like a powerful machine. Many machines have a variable speed control slider that allows you to set your speed where you want it.

To determine the amount of power you require for your sewing machine, think about the frequency and size of projects you will be stitching. You will want a slow stitch setting when you need precise stitches, but you'll love to stitch faster for straight stitches and for faster piecing. As your skills increase, you will appreciate a variety of speeds.

▶ **DARA'S TIP** *I find that when students are learning to quilt, they have better success when they increase the stitching speed.*

Throat Size

The distance between the needle and the base of the machine is called throat size. A standard sewing machine typically has a 6˝ throat, which is fine for most sewing. Free-motion quilting and many quilted projects are large and bulky and need more room between the needle and the base of the machine.

If you think you will be making full-size quilts, you might want to invest in a machine with a larger throat size; however, for quilting a baby-/lap-size quilt, a standard throat size is satisfactory.

Extension Table

An extension table slides on to the sewing machine to create a wider work surface, making it easier to maneuver a quilt under and around the needle. It is also helpful to have a place for your left hand to rest.

For many machines, you can purchase an extension table. If your machine doesn't have an optional extension table, try modifying a desk or table so that you can lower the machine down far enough that the needle is flush with the table.

Feed Dogs

Feed dogs are the metal teethlike grips located in the faceplate of the machine below the needle. They move back and forth, helping to push the fabric through the machine during stitching. There is much debate in the free-motion quilting (FMQ) world as to whether the feed dogs need to be disengaged or engaged during free-motion quilting. In the Chapter 4 skills workouts Bonus Assignments (page 40), there are several tasks designed to help you feel the difference when quilting with or without the feed dogs engaged. I personally keep my feed dogs engaged when free-motion quilting because my machine runs more efficiently when they are. Please experiment and decide what works best for you!

NEEDLES AND BOBBINS

Needle Type

Choosing the most appropriate needle minimizes stitching problems and makes your stitching experience more enjoyable!

All the professional free-motion quilters that I know use a *topstitch needle* for piecing and quilting, because ...

... the tip of the needle is sharp, but not so sharp that it slices the fabric.

... the eye of the needle is long, which reduces friction on the thread that might cause the thread to fray, split, or break.

... it has a longer groove, or *channel*, for the thread to nestle in, again to reduce friction.

Reducing the amount of friction reduces thread fraying and breaking which makes for a much happier quilter.

Needle Size

There are two numbers, metric and nonmetric, associated with needle size. The most popular needles are 70/10, 80/12, 90/14, and 100/16. As the numbers get bigger, so do the size of the eye and the groove.

Pairing the correct needle size with the type of thread (see Thread Weight, page 23) you plan to use reduces thread breakage and thread tension troubles. For most general quilting, an 80/12 topstitch needle is suitable.

· *For 40- to 50-weight thread*, use medium to large diameter needles (80/12 and 90/14).

· *For 60-weight thread*, use smaller diameter needles (70/10).

· *For 30-weight and lower thread*, use larger diameter needles (90/14 and 100/16).

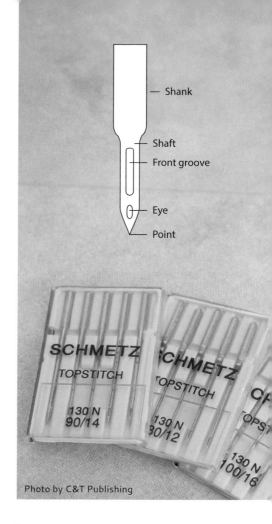

Photo by C&T Publishing

▶ **DARA'S TIP** *Change your needle every 8 hours or when you start a new project. However, titanium coated needles, although they are more expensive, last up to 60 hours longer! If you are worried about trying to keep track of the 60 hours of sewing time before the needle becomes dull, listen for a dull noise as the needle penetrates the fabric. When you hear the noise, it's time for a new needle.*

Bobbins

Bobbins hold the lower thread. I start every project by winding the number of bobbins I think I'll need to finish the project. There is no exact science that tells you how many bobbins you'll need to wind; however, as you become more accustomed to quilting your own projects, your guessing will become more accurate! If the quilting is dense and extends over a large area, you need more bobbins. Seeing if I wound enough bobbins for every project has been a little a game I always play, and I am always super-pleased when I get it right! Having bobbins ready to go is fundamental.

Prewound Bobbins

Prewound bobbins are wound in a factory and are sold ready to go. They hold 15%–40% more thread than the bobbins you wind yourself so you can stitch longer without stopping and they help minimize tension problems. The disadvantage to prewounds is that they are only available in limited colors, making it hard to match the top and bottom threads.

My favorite reason for using prewound bobbins—more sewing time because I don't have to keep stopping to change the bobbin!

Photo by C&T Publishing

PRESSER FEET

Your sewing machine comes with a standard presser foot, which can be used for straight stitch quilting; however, a walking foot is a helpful addition to your quilting supply stash and a darning foot is necessary for most free-motion quilting.

Walking Foot

A sewing machine has feed dogs (page 12) that help push the fabric forward during stitching. A walking foot, also called an *even-feed foot*, has its own set of feed dogs that rest on top of the fabric, to better move the multiple layers of the quilt evenly through the machine. This foot helps reduce puckering.

There are some generic walking feet; however, it is important to use the right walking foot for your machine. Although they all perform the same function, they can look different. Refer to your owner's manual for guidance and for how to attach a walking foot.

Also, some machines have "built-in" even-feed capability, so that a walking foot isn't necessary. Talk to your sewing machine dealer or read your manual for more about this.

Darning Foot

Most free-motion stitching is done with a darning foot. It has a spring which allows you to stitch randomly all over the quilt. The needle is completely at the mercy of the movements you make with your hands to maneuver the stitching all over the fabric.

There are generic darning feet, but if possible try to use a darning foot specific to your machine. If the foot is not made specifically for your machine, it might rest too close to the fabric, which adds extra pressure to the quilt layers and impedes free movement. If the darning foot you have is longer than it should be, raise the spring with an elastic band to reduce its length. Refer to your instruction manual.

I have a clear darning foot with a metal rim that I like to use as a guide for spacing and for echoing my designs. An open toe foot can be more liberating when creating other designs. I would recommend trying a variety to see what you prefer.

DRAWING IMPLEMENTS AND WRITING SURFACES

Another thing I like to teach my students when I am promising free–motion quilting success is the importance of doodling or sketching. It helps with muscle memory development and it's fun.

Muscle Memory Development

I like to call this skill doodling because it sounds a lot less ominous and daunting than sketching. Artists sketch, and I do not classify myself as an artist; rather, I see myself as a quilter. I recommend that you purchase a sketch book so all your doodles are in the same place. I often go back to my books and get ideas from previous doodles.

▶ **DARA'S TIP** *One of the first things we all learn at school is how to print, and then how to write in cursive. Because muscle memory is so important when quilting, practice cursive writing on a quilt. You can practice writing in cursive on fabric scraps and then stitching in cursive on a quilt sandwich (see Making a Quilt Sandwich, page 33).*

Drawing Implements

The two most popular pens for doodling are ballpoint and felt tip pens.

The number indicated on the pen refers to the size of the ball controlling the flow of ink, and thus the width of the lines the pens make. To better understand the numbering system a 0.5mm pen creates a line that is 0.5mm wide. The average pen size is about 1mm. Experiment with different pens to see which you find most comfortable.

▶ **DARA'S TIP** *The better the ink flow, the less likely your hands will cramp. The fine-tip Crayola marker is a great one for practicing but the tip is not as fine for the detail work of some of my doodles. I used to love the 0.5mm pens, but now that I have experimented I feel that the 0.7mm pens allow more flow and less cramping while not compromising the detail work of the quilt design.*

Writing Surfaces

Paper

There are all different grades of paper. I prefer a smooth paper that isn't so thick that you need to press harder, potentially resulting in hand fatigue.

White Boards

Drawing on white boards is a good idea because it is so smooth. The pen glides easily, which reduces fatigue. However, your hand might smudge your drawings and the only way to save your creations is by taking a photograph.

Notebooks

I love my doodle notebooks! They record my ideas and I find I go back to them often and for several reasons:

1. I see my progress.

2. I get inspiration from my doodles.

3. My doodles can be a jumping off point for another design.

4. I write ideas down that I might otherwise forget.

5. I celebrate the process of being creative and document it for further endeavors.

▶ **DARA'S TIP** *I buy packing paper from U-Haul to practice new designs. I sketch out the block or a portion of the quilt and practice drawing. Not only does this help me see if I like my design, but it helps establish the flow for the design so when I start stitching I will have fewer stops and starts. It helps to draw on a larger sheet to see the design on a real-life scale.*

UNDERSTANDING SEWING MACHINE TENSION

It is very important to have proper thread tension or your stitches won't be as strong as they should be. It is easiest to adjust the needle tension with either a dial or the touch screen of many electronic machines (see needle tension regulator). You can also adjust the bobbin tension, but it is a bit trickier (see bobbin tension). Regardless, when adjusting tension, make a single small adjustment at a time and then make a practice seam to check that you have corrected the issue.

When your needle and thread tension is set correctly, the stitches interlock between the fabric layers. ▶ **FIG.A**

When the top tension is too tight or the bobbin tension too loose, the bobbin thread will be pulled to the top of the fabrics. In this case, as a first step, **loosen the top thread tension.** ▶ **FIG.B**

When the top tension is too loose or the bobbin tension is too tight, the needle thread is pulled to the bottom fabric and you can feel the bobbin thread on the bottom of the quilt. In this case, as a first step, **tighten the top thread tension.** ▶ **FIG.C**

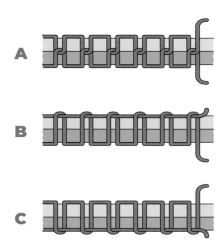

Tension Test

When you plan to free-motion quilt, test your tension on a quilt sandwich. Start with the needle tension set at 0 and keep adjusting the setting upward until the stitches look perfect. Most quilters will find that their settings usually fall between 2 and 3.5.

If the density of the quilt sandwich or the thickness of the thread changes, you might need to change the tension settings. Just remember: 0 (zero) is the loosest setting and 10 is the tightest. Refer to your instruction manual and experiment.

If you find you have tension issues, rethread the machine first, then reinstall the bobbin,

and finally try a new or different size needle. If these easy steps don't work, adjust the tension a tiny bit at a time and try stitching again. If you are still having issues, you might want to take your machine to your dealer for a cleaning and routine maintenance inspection.

▶ **DARA'S TIP** *My handy reference for solving tension issues is TNT: thread, needle, tension—in that order! I learned this from a fellow longarm quilter.*

Adjusting Tension

Always rethread the machine before adjusting the needle or bobbin tension.

Needle Tension Regulator

The tension regulator—two metal discs, sometimes hidden behind the machine's cover—allows you to change the needle thread tension (see your instruction manual). When sewing with thicker or heavier thread, you need to lower the tension setting and vice versa, you need to increase the tension setting for thinner threads. The varying thicknesses of thread makes such a difference when the thread travels through the tension disks and certainly is something to keep in mind as you expand your thread use.

Bobbin Tension

Refer to the instruction manual for specific information since typically you won't need to adjust the bobbin tension.

MAINTENANCE

All sewing machines require cleaning on a regular basis; lint and small threads are a natural byproduct of working with fibers and they tend to build up inside the machine. I find it most important to clean underneath and around the bobbin case.

Refer to your owner's manual for specific cleaning and maintenance information, particularly about the need and/or frequency to oil the machine.

▶ **DARA'S TIP** *Don't worry if you misplaced your owner's manual. I have had success looking them up online.*

A Maintenance Calendar

Here is one simple and important rule of thumb: Brush around the bobbin casing with every bobbin change!

Every Week

- Bend a pipe cleaner into the shape of a quarter and swipe around the inside and outside of the machine to remove dust and small threads.

- You can also use a piece of batting to dust around the outside of the machine.

- Cover your machine when you are not using it to minimize dust.

Every Month

- Take off the face plate and clean around the feed dogs.

- Oil the locations as indicated in the owner's manual.

- A can of compressed air is useful for cleaning inside the machine, but try not to blow lint further into the machine.

Every Year

- Depending on the usage, take your machine for a tune-up to a trusted sewing machine technician.

CHAPTER 2

Thread, Fabric, and Batting

My husband and I recently built onto our home for a studio. We used the straightest boards and all the best materials because we wanted to make sure that our studio addition would be perfect. Similarly, to guarantee success with your quilt, it is important to have some basic knowledge about the fabrics, threads, and batting that go into your quilt. Choose the best quality products that you can afford.

One of my first quilts was a disaster because I did not use the correct weight of thread for the size of needle I was using. Learn now so you do not have to suffer through my steep learning curve!

THREAD

There are so many kinds of thread, created from fibers such as cotton, polyester, silk, and wool. Finding the right thread was challenging for me when I first started free-motion quilting and I spent a lot of time trying different threads and practicing with different combinations of threads and needles. I learned that thread knowledge gives you sewing power!

Thread Weight

The most popular thread weights for piecing and quilting are 40-weight and 50-weight threads: 40-weight threads are slightly heavier and 50-weight threads are thinner and ideal for most quilting.

The Right Weight Thread for Quilting

50-weight thread is my go-to thread for free-motion quilting (I also use it for piecing) because it blends well with most fabrics. This weight is ideal for contrast stitching because the thread doesn't appear overwhelming, and it stitches easily through multiple fabric layers with very little lint buildup.

60-weight thread is often used in the bobbin because it is finer than 50-weight thread, you can fit more on the bobbin for extended sewing time. It doesn't produce a lot of lint and is ideal for stitching in the ditch when you want a blending thread. This weight of thread is also super for very close quilting when your pattern features intense fills.

100-weight thread is super-thin and is meant for micro quilting; it helps reduce bulk.

Thread Ply

Ply refers to the number of strands twisted together to make the thread. Look at the labels on your cones of thread and you will probably see a number like 50/3. The "50" refers to the *weight* of the thread and the "3" refers to the *number of strands*, or the *ply*.

If you are choosing between two threads, one labeled 50/2 and the other labeled 50/3, the 3-ply thread is thicker and stronger.

How many plies make up one thread?

▶ **DARA'S TIP**
How Thread is Wound on the Spool

Can you tell me the pattern of the thread sitting on your machine right now? Does the thread crisscross or is it wound parallel? Did you know that the way the thread is wound greatly effects the way it behaves when it comes off the spool during stitching?

As a rule of thumb, if the thread is wound on the spool crisscross, the thread needs to be lifted off the spool through an extended arm to help release the twist. If the threads are parallel they can be unwound straight off the cone or spool.

Types of Thread

Thread choice is often a matter of personal prefer- ence. Cotton, polyester, monofilament, metallic, and silk threads are suitable for most types of quilting. Although cotton thread is very strong and a favorite of many quilters, I prefer polyester thread for most of my quilting work.

Cotton

Cotton thread is strong, smooth, it doesn't stretch, and it is heat resistant, making it a good choice for quilting because of all the pressing required in the making of quilts. Some cotton thread is coated or glazed and should not be used for machine quilting.

▶ **DARA'S TIP** *Avoid thread that creates lint. Lint is composed of tiny bits of fabric and thread fibers. It can buildup in the machine mechanisms and cause problems with the tension and the operation of the machine.*

Polyester

Polyester is smooth, virtually lint free, and strong without being bulky. However, you do need to watch the heat setting on your iron; if the iron is too hot, it could possibly melt the thread.

Cotton versus Polyester Thread: An Experiment

Take time to become familiar with cotton and polyester threads. Cut a 12˝ length of 100% cotton thread and the same of 100% polyester thread. Which do you think is stronger?

· Break the polyester strand with your hands.

· Break the cotton strand with your hands.

Monofilament

Monofilament (polyester) thread is the closest you can get to invisible thread and comes in two colors, clear and smoky gray, to accommodate light and dark fabrics.

Metallic

Metallic thread has the shine of real metal in shades of silver, gold, bronze, and copper in pale and bright variations. This thread can have a spectacular effect as it glitters and shines; however, achieving the proper thread tension can be difficult (see Understanding Sewing Machine Tension, page 20).

Silk

Silk thread, while more expensive than the other threads, is very strong, smooth, and lint-free. It is colorfast with a beautiful natural sheen; it is available in vibrant colors and in various weights.

Nylon

Nylon thread should not be used for quilting or sewing.

How to Select the Best Thread for the Job

It is a good idea to spend time experimenting with a variety of threads. I invite you to make a practice quilt sandwich, put on your headphones with some of your favorite music, and allow yourself to enjoy thread experimentation. Be sure to adjust the stitch length and thread tension to determine the best combinations and take notes! You might even want to write the thread type and machine settings right on the quilt sandwich.

A few questions to consider:

1. Do I want the stitching to show?

2. What is the main purpose of my quilting project—decorative or functional?

3. Do I have the correct needle size for the weight of thread I am using?

▶ **DARA'S TIP** *Here is my recipe for success— 50-weight, 3-ply thread, with a topstitch needle size 90/14! My favorite thread is Superior So Fine! #50 and I use it 90% of the time.*

FABRIC

There are so many beautiful, incredible fabrics suitable for free-motion quilting. My healthy fabric stash attests to the fact that fabrics are really hard to resist. This brief run-down on different fabrics will provide some guidance as you begin and expand your free-motion quilting skills. A bit of fabric knowledge helps make fabric choice decisions easier. Always select the best quality fabric you can afford to avoid bleeding dyes, excessive shrinkage, and disappointing durability.

Cotton fabrics are available in a tremendous variety of both prints and solid colors. Prints tend to hide your stitching (useful when you are just starting) and solid color fabrics highlight your stitching designs.

Denim is usually medium-to-heavyweight and so it requires a strong needle (80/12).

Many denim fabrics shrink, so this is an important fabric to prewash.

Flannel is soft and cuddly, although it tends to shrink. Take the time to prewash the yardage before you start cutting.

Minky is soft, cuddly, and silky soft; it has nap, so make sure you cut all your pieces in the same direction. This fabric comes wide and extrawide (58˝–60˝), perfect for quilt backing; it stretches; it is quite slippery (so spray baste and/or use a lot of pins); and it doesn't shrink. Because of the slippery stretch factors, use a walking foot and slightly larger seam allowance (½˝ instead of ¼˝) when piecing.

Polar fleece is similar to Minky in that it stretches, but doesn't shrink. It tends to be thick, so you might need to adjust the height of the needle. (Refer to your sewing machine manual.)

Silk fabrics are super-luxurious, but rather delicate to sew. Use a fine needle (60/8 or 70/10) and increase the upper thread tension.

- If you think your fabric might shrink or the dyes might bleed, definitely prewash it before cutting. Not all fabrics are the same quality.

- Long staple, tightly woven cottons shrink less than loosely woven varieties.

- If there is a high contrast of colors, particularly shades of red mixed with white, prewash! There are products, such as Shout Color Catchers, that reduce color bleeding.

- Always prewash flannel and denim (unless you are making a rag quilt and want frayed edges).

- If you want a slightly wrinkled "antique" look, don't prewash the fabric.

BATTING

Batting is the "fluffy stuff" between the top and bottom of the quilt. There are many types of batting, each serving a unique purpose. When you select batting, consider the purpose of the quilt, where the quilt will be used, and how thick or heavy you want the quilt to be. Review the batting varieties listed here to choose the one right for your project.

Bamboo batting is fairly new to the quilting world. It is a natural fiber made from renewable resources; it is durable, antibacterial, and breathable. It can be quilted between ¼˝ and 8˝ apart.

Cotton batting is warm and breathable. It has medium loft and can be quilted between ½˝ and 4˝ apart. It is suitable for both hand and machine quilting.

Cotton/polyester batting is usually a mix of 80% cotton and 20% polyester. The combination of polyester and cotton fibers increases the strength of the batting, so quilts can undergo a lot of love and use. It can be quilted from ¼˝ to 4˝ apart. This batting is, by far, my go-to batting for my own quilts and those I make for my clients.

Polyester batting has increased my appreciation for polyester! It doesn't shrink, is available in a variety of thicknesses (referred to as loft), is relatively inexpensive, and can be quilted from ¼˝ to 4˝ apart.

Silk batting makes a soft and supple natural fiber batting. It drapes beautifully and is very lightweight. It is wonderful for hand or machine quilting on both quilts and garments. This batting can be quilted from ¼˝ to 4˝ apart.

Wool batting has a very high loft that showcases a quilter's piecing and stitching. When I want my free-motion quilting to stand out, I quilt with a layer of wool on top and a layer of cotton/polyester (80/20) batting on the bottom. Wool is lightweight and breathable; it provides warmth in cold weather but is cool enough for hot tropical and humid climates! Most wool batting can be washed gently in a washing machine and hung to dry. Wool batting can be quilted from ¼˝ to 4˝ apart.

CHAPTER 3

Setting up Your Space and Setting Goals

To ensure success, know how to set up a physical sewing space for free-motion quilting, minimize hand and body fatigue, and set personal goals. Thankfully we are all different and so are our space and time limitations, so here are some recommendations that work for me. I would love your feedback on how these are ideas are working for you!

PHYSICAL SPACE

There are many things to consider when setting up a quilting area. It is important to have a large surface for cutting fabric and planning your quilt or project design. It is equally important that you can lay out your pinned project on an extended surface while free-motion quilting, so the pinned fabrics don't fall off the work surface and distort your stitching. If possible, create an L-shape with another table so that the machine can be on one table and the bulk of the quilt can lie on the other table. This helps spread out the quilt and distribute the weight. (See Extension Table, page 11.)

For a queen-size quilt, the recommended surface area is 4 ft. × 5 ft.

Organization

Keep your quilting supplies together and nearby to minimize time spent looking for things and to reduce distractions.

Lighting

Good lighting is essential so you are can see what you are quilting. If the space where you are working does not have adequate light, bring in extra light. You might consider purchasing a specialized light that fits on or near your sewing machine to illuminate your sewing area. You can also experiment with setting up your work station closer to a window for natural light.

Minimizing Hand and Body Fatigue

Guiding the three layers of the quilt project through your machine can be a rewarding experience when your brain connects with your body as you make the movements for free-motion quilting. I find that by raising my chair I do not have to raise my arms up as high; I have a higher vantage point so I can see better; and I sit taller with less strain on my shoulders. It is important to be mindful about how you feel while quilting and make changes if you are not comfortable. Take breaks, set a timer to remind yourself to stand up, and stretch. This is a physical activity. Every 15 minutes or so, lean back, arch your back, and roll your shoulders.

Quilting Gloves

I am a huge advocate for wearing gloves while quilting because it adds grip and control to the quilting project. I prefer Machinger gloves. They come in various sizes, and most importantly, they have grips on all five finger tips which provide a lot of control with very little pressure. One of the biggest problems I see with beginner free-motion quilters is that when they shift the quilt project under their needle they are holding too tight. This tightness travels up the arms into the shoulders which can lead to headaches. Only your fingertips and sides of your hands should be touching the fabric.

SETTING GOALS

"Setting goals is the first step in turning the invisible into visible." —Tony Robbins

I encourage my students to focus on the process of learning rather than the outcome or final results. One of the most important aspects of learning how to free-motion quilt is to commit yourself to learning. It is equally important to avoid frustration by accepting imperfection.

Stephen Covey said, "Begin with the end in mind." It is important to set personal goals. Goals help:

· Provide focus.

· Measure progress.

· Stay on task.

· Overcome procrastination.

· Provide motivation

Try to work quilting into your schedule every day—even if you simply doodle. This book is designed to help you set goals and work towards accomplishing them with practice exercises and simple projects.

Finding Support

We often turn to quilting for alone time, although we need to be inspired and encouraged in our efforts. Quilting with others simply isn't possible on a day-to-day basis, so building a support system is very helpful. Consider the following, because quilters are some of the most wonderful people!

· Join a local guild to find helpful and encouraging support.

· Finding like-minded quilters online is also a great way to connect. Join Facebook groups, watch YouTube videos, and connect on Instagram to be inspired and to receive encouragement and support.

I enjoy posting videos on my YouTube channel, hosting live lessons on Instagram and Facebook, blogging, and teaching in person to connect with others. (See Resources, page 140.)

A Quilter's Log

Feel free to copy this page for your personal use or simply create your own log with this as a guide.

KEY TO QUILTER'S LOG

Goals: What you wish to accomplish

Action plan: Your timeline breakdown

Progress report: On a scale of 1 to 10, how do you feel about your progress?

Reflection: How you are progressing; pros and cons

Notes: Things you want to remember

PROJECT:

Goals:

Action plan:

Progress report:

Reflection:

Notes:

CHAPTER 4

Basic Skills

One of the most important aspects of learning how to free-motion quilt is to commit yourself to learning and realize that accepting imperfection is part of the process.

BASICS OF FREE-MOTION QUILTING

Making a quilt takes a lot of time and effort, so many quilters are fearful of ruining their quilts if they make a mistake while free-motion quilting. I understand that! I have spent many hours unpicking, but I have also decided that I need to be kind to myself and be happy with where I am with my skills. So be kind to yourself. Invest in yourself with practice and skill development. Take the workouts seriously and do them. Your practice will pay off and the results will be very rewarding.

1. Get out a quilt sandwich and "warm-up" for 5 minutes or so. Check the tension, thread delivery, needle size, and general stitch quality. Be sure to check the bottom side of the sandwich, too.

2. Decide whether you prefer to stitch with the feed dogs up or down (see Feed Dogs, page 12).

3. Always try to start quilting at one of the edges. If you need to start in the center, remember to anchor the stitches by taking 4 or 5 stitches in place or by burying the threads after you finish stitching.

▶ **DARA'S TIP** *There is considerable debate in the quilting world about the importance of burying thread knots in the middle of the quilt; it is rather tedious!*

To bury knots:

1. Bring the bottom thread up to the top of the quilt.

2. Tie the bottom and top threads together so a knot forms close to the quilt top.

3. Thread both threads through a needle (use a self-threading needle to make this easy!), and insert the needle back in the last stitch hole through the top fabric, the batting, and then out again about ½˝ away. Be careful not to run the threads through the backing.

4. Tug on the thread to bring the knot through the top fabric and the batting.

5. Trim the thread ends close to where they were pulled through the quilt top.

4. Before starting, check the suggested maximum distance to leave between rows or shapes of stitching. This information is determined by the type of batting you are using. Refer to the information about batting (page 27) for guidance.

5. As you move the quilt under the machine, use the tips of your fingers and the light touch of the exterior palm of your hand to guide the fabric where you want it to go.

6. Look ahead, don't look at the presser foot; plan for where you want to quilt before starting to stitch. Visualize your design.

7. Remember to relax your shoulders!

▶ **DARA'S TIP** *If your sewing machine has a needle–up/down feature, adjust it to "needle down" when free-motion quilting so that when you stop to shift your hands the fabric doesn't shift.*

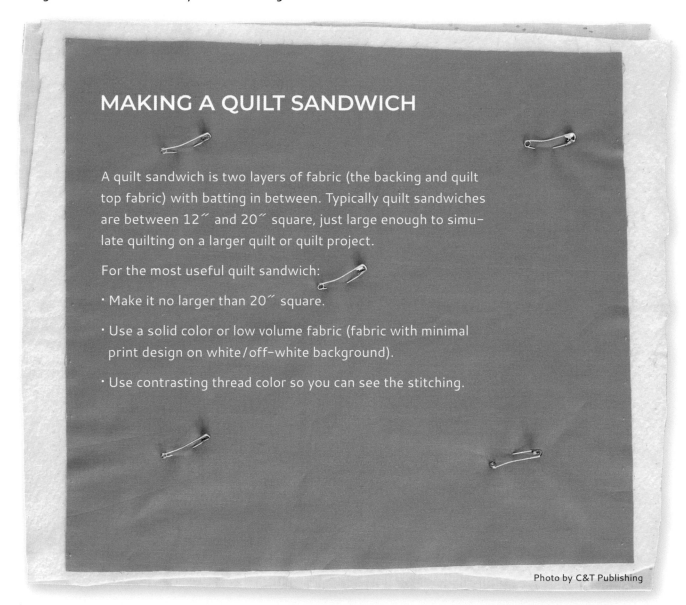

MAKING A QUILT SANDWICH

A quilt sandwich is two layers of fabric (the backing and quilt top fabric) with batting in between. Typically quilt sandwiches are between 12″ and 20″ square, just large enough to simulate quilting on a larger quilt or quilt project.

For the most useful quilt sandwich:

· Make it no larger than 20″ square.

· Use a solid color or low volume fabric (fabric with minimal print design on white/off–white background).

· Use contrasting thread color so you can see the stitching.

Photo by C&T Publishing

I am a huge advocate of quilt sandwiches because they allow you to practice free-motion techniques, audition new designs, and refine your abilities. I save all the batting pieces I have left over from my large quilts and separate them into two groups: 12″ pieces for rag quilts and larger pieces for quilt sandwiches and/or for smaller quilts.

▶ **DARA'S TIP** *To make your quilt sandwich extra useful, use one color of thread to practice your FMQ and then change thread color for a second round of stitching practice. By changing the color of thread, you can reuse the same quilt sandwich.*

▶ **DARA'S TIP** *If you are like me and don't like waste, why not serge around the edges of your quilt sandwiches and take them down to your local SPCA or zoo where these soft mats can be used to care for the animals?*

BASTING A QUILT

Basting a quilt is the process of temporarily securing the backing, batting, and quilt top together so the layers don't shift during the quilting process.

- The quilt backing should be at least 4″ larger all around than the quilt top.

- The quilt batting should be at least 3″ larger all around than the quilt top.

For example: If the quilt top is 40″ × 40″, the backing should be 48″ × 48″ and the batting should be 46″ × 46″. The backing and batting need to be wider than the quilt top so you have a place to position your hands when you are machine quilting the edges.

Note: The backing and batting may require piecing two or more pieces of fabric (or batting) to obtain the necessary width and length.

Preparing and Laying Out the Backing

1. Prepare a clean, flat surface (or wall) for laying out the quilt. Position the backing, right side down on the surface. Be sure to smooth away any wrinkles.

▶ **DARA'S TIP** *You can baste your quilt on the floor, on a large table, or on a wall.*

2. With 1″-wide tape—painters or masking tape for cotton and clear packing tape for Minky or polar fleece (stretchy polyester backings)—secure the backing to the surface as follows.

a. Cut several 5″ strips of tape. Attach the tape parallel to the edge of the fabric. Do not pull on or stretch the fabric, but the fabric needs to be taut so there are no wrinkles on the back.

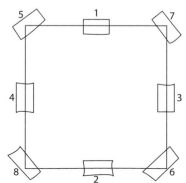

b. Tape the bottom and top center.

c. Tape the top right corner and then the bottom left corner.

d. Tape the top left corner and then the bottom right corner.

e. Depending on the size of the quilt that you are basting, continue in this manner until there are only 3″–4″ gaps between pieces of tape.

f. Locate the middle of each side of the backing and mark it with a line on the tape or a pin.

3. Pin or spray baste the backing, batting, and quilt top layers together, following the instructions below.

Pin Basting or Spray Basting

Try both pin and spray basting, both methods work well. It is really a matter of personal preference which method you decide to use.

Pin Basting

There are special quilt basting pins that have a bend in the arm that make it easier to rock the pin through the quilt layers.

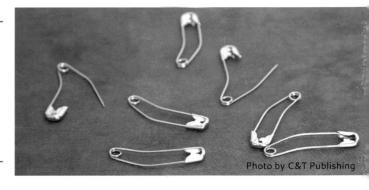

Photo by C&T Publishing

1. Before pinning the quilt, decide on the free-motion quilting plan. Knowing how the quilt will be stitched helps you know where to place the pins. For example, if you plan to stitch-in-the-ditch (page 42), do not pin along any seams because the pins will interrupt the flow of quilting.

2. Center and then layer the batting over the backing. Smooth to remove any wrinkles.

3. Locate the middle of each side of the quilt top and then place it, right side up, on top of the backing and batting. Line up the centers of the top and backing that you've marked.

4. Secure the pins starting in the middle and working toward the edges. Pin every 5″. Continue to smooth the top while pinning.

5. Make sure that the quilt top doesn't move as you pin. It is very frustrating if the quilt top shifts and you have to remove the pins and start over because the top is not flat or it doesn't align with the batting and backing.

▶ **DARA'S TIP** *I like to scatter my pins around the quilt to make sure I have enough of them, before I start the basting. This is also very handy because the pins are at my fingertips and easy to reach during the process.*

Spray Basting

Spray basting is my preference because it is so speedy and if the quilt top shifts and I have made a mistake, I can simply peel off the top and try again. I go through the same basic process of securing the backing, but then I spray the wrong sides of the backing and the quilt top.

▶ **DARA'S TIP** *My favorite spray baste is Odif 505 Spray and Fix Temporary Fabric Adhesive. I find that I don't need a lot of spray because it is very effective.*

1. Once the backing is secure, lay out the quilt top right side down on the backing. Spray the quilt top so that the over-spray is caught by the backing. Do not spray the batting, the spray baste is absorbed and is wasted.

2. Carefully remove the quilt top and spray the wrong side of the backing fabric. Place the batting in the center of the backing, smoothing it out. Center and smooth the quilt top over the layers, pressing the layers together with your hands. If there are wrinkles, lift off the quilt top and tray again.

3. "Set" the spray by pressing the three layers together. If the backing is a polyester fabric such as Minky or polar fleece, press the cotton side only.

▶ **DARA'S TIP** *If you are spraying in your home, place newspapers around the backing to avoid too much mess on the floor. Ensure that there is adequate ventilation.*

▶ **DARA'S TIP** *There is one-sided adhesive batting available. Position the batting against the wrong side of the fabric and press with a hot iron to release the adhesive and secure the layers together. Keep in mind that the nonadhesive side still needs to be basted for free-motion quilting success.*

MAKING AND ATTACHING BINDING

How to Make Binding

1. Prepare the binding fabric by trimming the fabric edges and cutting away the selvages. It helps to use a rotary cutter and the longest quilter's ruler you have.

2. Cut the strips 2½˝ wide by the width of fabric (WOF), as shown in the project instructions.

3. Join the strips at a 45° angle to obtain the desired length of binding for the project as shown. ▶ **FIG.A**

4. Trim the seam allowances to ¼˝ and press the seams open. ▶ **FIG.B**

5. Continue joining all the strips in this manner until they are all connected.

6. Fold the strip in half lengthwise, right sides together, so it is 1¼˝ wide, and press.

How to Attach Binding

1. Attach the binding by lining up the raw edges of the binding with the raw edges of the quilt or project, right sides together. Start pinning the binding in place, about a third of the way down one side. Measure and use a pin to mark 10˝ from where you started pinning the binding.

2. Begin stitching at the 10˝ mark with ¼˝ seam allowance (The unstitched section of the beginning of the binding will be connected to the end of the binding later). Continue sewing to ¼˝ from the end of the first corner. With your needle in the down position, sew off the corner at a 45° angle. ▶ **FIG.C**

3. Fold the binding up at a 45° angle up away from the quilt, as shown. ▶ **FIG.D**

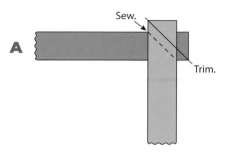

A — Sew. Trim.

B

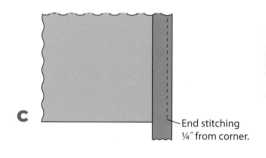

C — End stitching ¼˝ from corner.

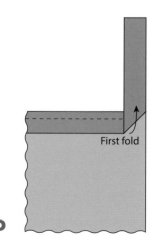

D — First fold

4. Make a second fold by bringing the binding straight down so the second fold lines up with the first (stitched) side of the project and the edges of the binding line up with the second edge of the project. ▶ **FIG.E**

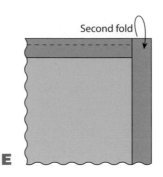

E

5. Continue to attach the binding to the quilt with a ¼˝ seam allowance until the next corner. Repeat Steps 2–4 at the remaining corners. Continue sewing until reaching the pin marking.

6. Take the quilt out from under the machine. Measure 2½˝ from the end of the binding strip and cut away any extra binding. ▶ **FIG.F**

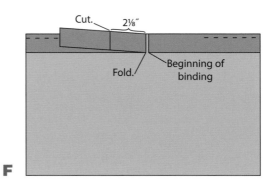

F

7. Unfold the unstitched ends of the binding strips and pin them right sides together at a right angle. Draw a line diagonally across the top strip and stitch along this line. Refold the binding strip and make sure it fits when you lay it along the unsewn portion of the quilt. If you like the fit, trim the seam allowance on the diagonal seam to ¼˝ and press open. ▶ **FIG.G**

8. Once the ends of the binding are joined, refold the binding, and stitch the edges to the project with a ¼˝ seam allowance. Be sure to backstitch at each end of the seam.

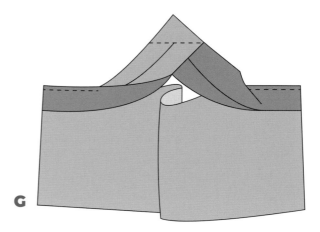

G

9. To finish binding the project, fold the finished edge of the binding over to the other side of the quilt, encasing the seam. Machine or hand stitch the binding in place.

QUILT LABELS: A SPECIAL TOUCH

I always have one or two quilts made and ready to be donated. My heart has been overwhelmed by the generosity of those who give so freely to help others in need. One of the main reasons I quilt is so that I can give my quilts away to people who might need them. My quilts are made and given with love and I believe that love stays in the heart of both the giver and receivers. I am so grateful for this way to increase love in this world. I am passionate about teaching and empowering others to take on this approach.

My go-to method for making quilt labels is purchasing preprinted labels, cutting them out, and raw edge appliquéing them to the finished quilt. Then, I use a permanent marker to write a message, my name, and the date.

You might want to design your own quilt labels or embroider your name or a message of love on the back in one of the quilt's corners. Be sure to add your signature somewhere so that your good works send your good thoughts to those who receive your gifts.

Quilt detail photo by Vanessa Lust Photography; quilt label photo by C&T Publishing

Foundation Building Practice Workouts

Try the following workouts to take you from stitch-walking to stitch-running in no time!

Date	Time	Task
		Take out all the needles in your sewing room and sort them by size and type. Do you have the correct needle sizes? Do you need to go to your local quilt shop and purchase new ones? Separate the FMQ needles from the other needles to reduce confusion in the future.
		Have a look through your thread stash. How old is the thread? If it is older than 10 years, do not use it for FMQ.
		Sort thread by size.
		Sort thread by ply.
		Make a quilt sandwich with 100% cotton fabric preferably in a solid color fabric, approximately 20″ square. Baste it with pins.
		Make a quilt sandwich with 100% cotton fabric preferably in a solid color fabric, approximately 20″ square and baste it with spray baste.
		Attach your walking foot. Starting in the middle, stitch one quilt sandwich by bringing the bottom thread up and secure the stitches. Continue to sew until about 1″ from the end of the sandwich; end the stitching by bringing the bottom thread up and securing the threads.
		With the walking foot still on the machine, stitch several lines going north to south, east to west, south to north, and west to east.
		With the walking foot on the machine, stitch several curved lines. Notice your stitch length—has it changed or remained the same?
		Put on the darning foot. Release the feed dogs. Pull your bottom thread up. Start stitching on the left side and make your way to the right side of the fabric for 5″. Change directions and stitch back and forth for 5 minutes. How does this feel?

BONUS ASSIGNMENTS

· With the darning foot on your machine engage the feed dogs and make your way from the right to the left side. Continuously stitch for 5 minutes—can you feel a difference with the feed dogs up?

· With the darning foot on your machine write your name with the feed dogs engaged. Now disengage the feed dogs and write your name. Compare the two.

DESIGN ELEMENTS AND PROJECTS

Each star on this quilt features one of the design elements highlighted in the following chapters. Just think what you can make once you learn and practice these beautiful free-motion quilting designs. For block instructions and to see the full quilt, see BONUS! Sawtooth Star Block (page 139).

CHAPTER 5

Straight-Line Quilting

WHAT YOU NEED

- Walking foot (see Walking Foot, page 15)

- Quilt sandwich, about 18˝ square

- Ruler

- Fabric marking pen

- Rotary cutter and cutting mat (*optional*)

Skills You Learn

- How to use a walking foot

- Stitching on a quilt sandwich

- Moving three layers of fabric under a needle

- Importance of quilting gloves

- Technique: Stitch-in-the-ditch

DESIGN ELEMENT: STRAIGHT LINES

Start thinking about straight lines in a whole different way. They can be so much more than stitching along an edge, or a seam, or in the ditch of a seam (see Stitch-in-the-Ditch, at right).

Prepare a quilt sandwich (see Making a Quilt Sandwich, page 33) to learn about straight-line designs. Use a ruler and marking pen to divide the quilt sandwich into three equal sections and then divide those in half, each measuring roughly 6˝ × 9. We'll use 5 sections and there will be an extra section for you to do with what you wish—perhaps creating your own variation!

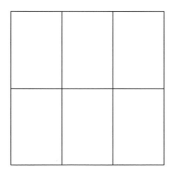

Stitch-in-the-Ditch: A Straight-Line Quilting Technique

This is the practice of stitching directly over the seams of a quilt top to anchor the three layers of the quilt together. When I first started quilting, I always stitched in all the ditches! This gave me great confidence as I successfully maneuvered the three layers of the quilt through my sewing machine. Eventually my confidence increased and I started to branch out from stitching over every seam. I also started using a walking foot.

Design Variations

1. In the first section, stitch long columns back and forth approximately ½˝ apart. Keep the needle down when turning. How does this feel? ▶ **FIG.A**

2. Staggered lines create a different and fresh look. In the second section, stitch irregularly spaced lines both vertically and horizontally, as shown. Don't be afraid to trace the lines with your finger to follow the movement. ▶ **FIG.B**

3. Make the lines cross. Imagine that you are playing on a pinball machine, but that the ball leaves a stitch behind it every new way it moves. Perhaps taking a ruler and drawing diagonal lines back and forth on a piece of paper can help you picture this design. I like to experiment with the density of lines, the angles of the lines, and the variety of the design. ▶ **FIG.C**

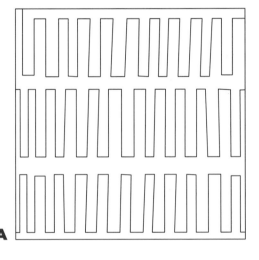

A

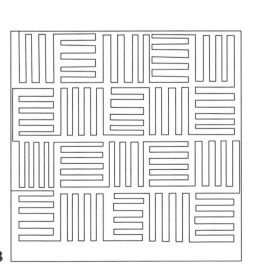

B

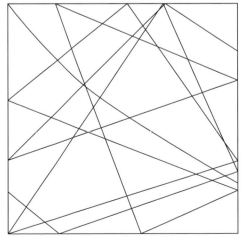

C

4. The classic herringbone design can be achieved by combining the previous designs. First, stitch the center columns in the desired width. After those are stitched, starting from the upper left corner, angle your stitches down to the first column. Once you have reach that line, angle back up toward the next column. This creates the baseline for the rest of your design. Continue stitching back and forth, echoing the previously stitched out design. ▶ **FIG.D**

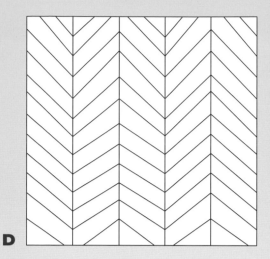

D

5. This design helps with spatial awareness. Create a "square" swirl and then stitch your way back out of the swirl. Watch where your walking foot is in relation to the previously stitched line. Experiment with various widths. ▶ **FIG.E**

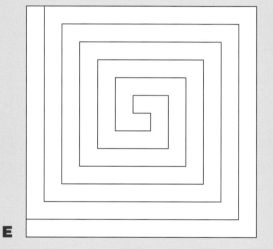

E

Practice Workouts

Date	Time	Task
		Use a pen and paper to draw a row of squares side by side without lifting the pen. It's okay to go back over a previously-drawn line.
		Draw three separate rectangles approximately 15˝ × 3˝. In each rectangle draw different designs without lifting the writing utensil. Challenge yourself to create different designs.
		Draw one large rectangle in spiral and then spiral back to the top without lifting the writing utensil.
		Attach a walking foot to your sewing machine and recreate one of your drawings on a quilt sandwich.
		Use a walking foot and stitch to create three rectangles on a quilt sandwich. Practice starting and stopping stitching.
		Stitch to fill in the rectangles from the previous task, with three designs different from those you drew.
		On a 10˝ × 10˝ quilt sandwich, stitch to create four boxes that are approximately 5˝ square. In the first box, stitch horizontal lines. In the second box, stitch vertical lines. In the third box, stitch lines at a 45° angle that slant to the right. In the fourth box, stitch lines at a 45° angle that slant to the left.
		Draw a linear design onto a new quilt sandwich without lifting the pen. Then stitch over the line without lifting the needle.
		Prepare a 7˝ × 5˝ quilt sandwich to see how densely you can quilt straight lines. Set a timer for 10 minutes and quilt parallel lines without them touching.
		Use the 7˝ × 5˝ quilt sandwich from the previous task to recreate grid paper by stitching perpendicular to your first set of lines. Use the walking foot to keep the rows of stitching straight and parallel.

ON A ROLL
Pencil Holder

Finished pencil holder: Approximately 9˝ × 20˝

I inherited my grandma Hazel's knitting and crochet hooks. She had created a needle case that I cherish but the functionality of it was challenging because the needles did not always stay in place and they tended to slip out. By adding double strips of extrawide elastic to the case, my needles are secure. This led me to design the pencil roll!

MATERIALS AND SUPPLIES

Yardage is based on 44˝-wide fabric.

Backing fabric: ⅜ yard

Inside panel fabric: ⅓ yard

Binding: ¼ yard

Batting: 1 rectangle 10½˝ × 22˝

Colorful elastic: 2˝ wide,
2 pieces each 22˝ long

Ribbon: 1½˝ (or less) wide,
30˝ long

Colored pencils: 24 colors

CUTTING

Backing

- Cut 1 rectangle
  11˝ × 23˝.

Inside panel

- Cut 1 rectangle
  10˝ × 21˝.

Binding

- Cut 2 strips
  2¼˝ × WOF.

Batting

- Cut 1 rectangle
  10½˝ × 22˝.

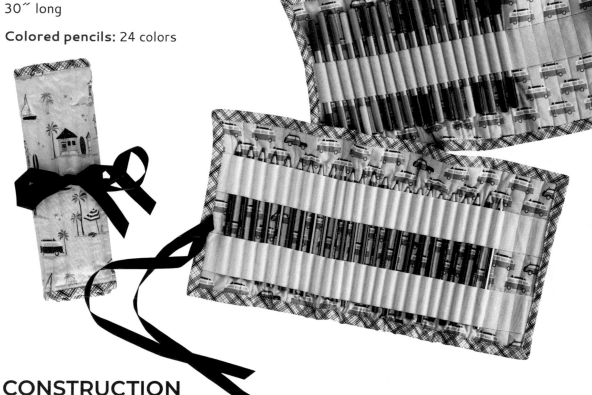

CONSTRUCTION

Seam allowances are ¼˝ unless otherwise noted.

▶ **DARA'S TIP** *The instructions that follow are for a pencil roll that holds 24 colored pencils. However, feel free to make it larger or smaller to create the size project you want. So, if you have paintbrushes, makeup brushes, or even a chopstick collection, resize the roll and make it your own! If you do make the pencil roll wider, you might want to add a second piece of elastic.*

Making the Pencil Roll

1. Prepare the quilt sandwich (see Making a Quilt Sandwich, page 33) with the inside panel, batting, and backing. Before basting, and with the inside panel facing up, place 1 or 2 pieces of elastic across the pencil roll, as shown. Pin and baste the short ends of the elastic along each side. Baste the pencil roll as desired with your preferred method. ▶ **FIG.A**

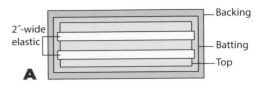

DARA'S TIP *If you are making a taller pencil roll, use two pieces of elastic to hold your tools or markers more snugly. A narrower pencil roll might only need one strip of elastic.*

2. Starting at one edge, use the quilting ruler and fabric marking pen to draw vertical stitching placement lines every ¾˝ across the entire quilt sandwich. Take care that the ruler is parallel to the edge of the pencil roll. There should be 27 placement lines to create 26 slots for the pencils. I like to have a couple extra slots for stray pencils or pens. ▶ **FIG.B**

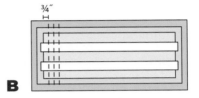

3. Attach the walking foot and stitch along the marked stitching lines, catching the elastic in the process.

▶ **DARA'S TIP** *It is better to sew each placement line from the top of the roll to the bottom. This minimizes puckering and wrinkles in the fabric.*

▶ **DARA'S TIP** *I like to reinforce the beginning and end of these stitching lines, by backstitching, for about 4 or 5 stitches. This helps strengthen the stretch/ pressure areas.*

Finishing

1. Trim the project with a rotary cutter and ruler to measure 9˝ × 20½˝.

2. Before attaching the binding, fold the ribbon in half. With the backing side facing up, pin the fold of the ribbon to the center of the left side of the pencil roll. Baste the fold in place so it will be caught in the binding. ▶ **FIG.C**

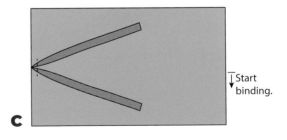

3. Prepare and attach the binding (see Making and Attaching Binding, page 37).

Your roll is ready for coloring projects anytime and anywhere!

Straight-Line Stitched Quilt

Finished quilt: 40″ × 61″

Straight-line free-motion quilting adds a special touch to this simple quilt. If you want to bring a quilt along with your pencil roll for a drawing session, make this quick quilt with coordinating fabrics for a trip to the beach or the sofa!

MATERIALS AND CUTTING

Yardage is based on 44″-wide fabric.

Fabric A: 1 yard
Cut 3 strips 10″ × WOF.

Fabric B: 1 yard
Cut 3 strips 10″ × WOF.

Border and binding: ⅞ yard
Cut 11 strips 2½″ × WOF.

Backing: 2⅔ yards

Batting: 48″ × 69″

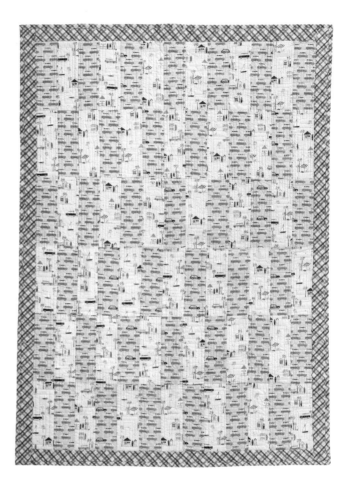

INSTRUCTIONS

Sew 3 strip sets with fabric A on top and press the seams downward. Subcut the strip sets into units 3½″ wide. Lay out the units as desired with 12 units across and 3 down. Sew the quilt top. *(Note: I had extrawide fabric and was able to cut 13 units from each strip set, so my quilt is 13 units across instead of 12.)*

Sew 3 of the border fabric strips together to create 1 long strip, and then subcut 2 strips each 61½″ long. Cut 2 more border strips 36½″ long. Sew the border strips to the top and bottom of the quilt front and then to the sides.

Baste the quilt—FMQ with lines of straight stitching—in- or out-of-the-ditch (see Stitch-in-the-Ditch, page 42)! Trim the edges and then make and attach the binding.

Quilting Directional e's and l's

WHAT YOU NEED

- Darning foot
- Quilt sandwich, 15˝ square
- Quilting ruler
- Marking pen
- Spray baste or basting pins
- Rotary cutter

Skills You Learn

- How to use a darning foot
- Stitching on a quilt sandwich
- Moving three layers of fabric under a needle
- Importance of quilting gloves
- Quilting a design along a prescribed line
- Spacing distance and height
- Mirroring a design

DESIGN ELEMENTS: E'S AND L'S

When many of us started school, we were taught the basic principles of letter formation. Although the practice of teaching handwriting is waning, many of us have had some training in cursive. We built our muscle memory of the letters with a lot of repetition. In fact, after a short time, writing cursive became natural and soon felt effortless.

1. Remember the scribblers with the dotted line exactly in the middle of the top and bottom lines? Imagine the same structure to draw the e's and l's. The l's are just taller e's. Start drawing the loops at the bottom left, curve up toward the top of the loop, curve the top, and then curve down to the lower right. And repeat. It really can be that simple once you put your mind to it. ▶ **FIG.A**

A

2. I suggest beginners practice with lined paper and turn the paper so the lines are going vertically. This provides help in spacing the "letters" or "design" evenly. The success of the design is achieved through a nice consistent look. ▶ **FIG.B**

3. Practice drawing l's on lined paper, they will be easy after mastering the e's. To make the "l," simply draw a longer reach before curving the top. ▶ **FIG.C**

4. The difference between the e's and the l's is the height of the loop; create a free-motion design pattern by alternating e's and l's. ▶ **FIG.D**

5. Leaning how to create the design in all directions is important for a quilter. Practice changing the direction of the loops. ▶ **FIG.E**

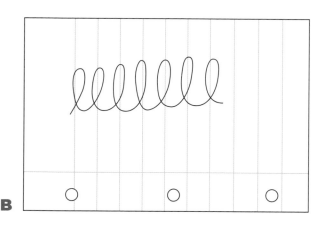

B

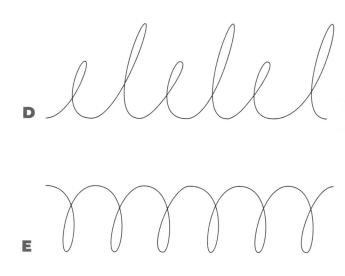

D

E

C

Design Variations

There are countless ways to vary designs with e's and l's. Try these five and then create a few of your own!

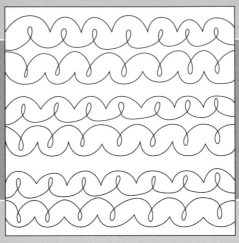

Lacey

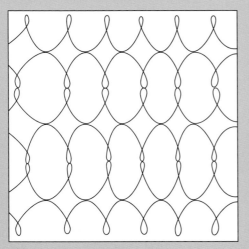

On-Point

Sound Waves

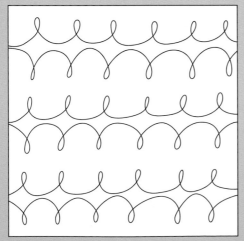

Opposites Attract

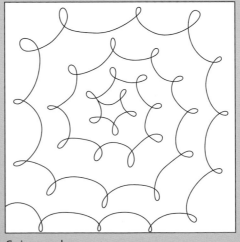

Spirograph

Practice Workouts

Date	Time	Task
		Draw e's on a lined sheet of paper. Continue drawing e's without lifting the pencil for 5 minutes.
		Fill a lined sheet of paper with continuous l's. Draw different size l's by drawing them on 1 line of the paper, or 2 lines of the paper, or even 3 lines of the paper.
		Alternate drawing continuous e's and l's in sequence for 2 minutes. Pay attention to the slope of the letters. They should be perpendicular. Then turn the lined paper so the lines are vertical and draw the e's and l's for another 2 minutes.
		On blank paper, draw 3 lines of e's and then 3 lines of l's one inch apart. Then mirror the lines by drawing the e's and l's upside down to develop muscle memory.
		Practice drawing different scale e's and l's. On blank paper, experiment creating e's and l's in all different sizes for 5 minutes.
		On blank paper, draw 3 lines of l's spaced apart ½″ apart and leave an inch or so between each line. Now go back and stagger the l's so they fit into the loops. Consider how they might look in your quilting?
		Practice drawing e's and l's to create designs of different density. The closer the e's and l's the denser the design appears. Set the timer for 5 minutes and experiment with drawing a variety of rows going from less to more dense. Don't forget to focus on even spacing!
		On grid paper, draw 3 rows of e's and l's. Review the spacing between the e's and l's. Remember in math class and how your teacher uses a mirror to teach about shapes that are symmetrical? This is the goal for sewing e's and l's.
		Make a quilt sandwich, set the timer for 5 minutes and sew continuous e's and l's. Do not worry about symmetry, just focus on flow.
		Create a design on the quilt sandwich. Take a picture and send it to me! I want to cheer your success.

TOTE-ALLY TERRIFIC
Tote Bag

Finished tote: 18˝ × 18˝ with 17˝ straps

One of the best organizing tips I ever read when I became a mother was to have a tote for every event in which I was involved. For example, to be organized for book club, have a designated tote and keep all book club material in there; if you are a member of a community association keep all

papers and information in a designated tote; and if you are part of carpool for school-related or athletic events, keep a tote for snacks, contact information, and the driving schedule. Although I am an organized person in general, this concept was empowering for me since I seem to wear many hats!

During the construction of this tote bag, you'll learn how to make a gusset for the bag bottom, how to make padded straps, and how to add a lining that features a perfect extra pocket.

MATERIALS AND SUPPLIES

Yardage is based on 44″-wide fabric.

Exterior fabrics:
3 coordinating fabrics for tote exterior and straps

  Fabric A: ½ yard

  Fabric B: ½ yard

  Fabric C: ½ yard

Lining: ⅔ yard

Backing: ⅔ yard (This will be hidden by the lining, so you can use muslin.)

Pocket: 6½″ × 12½″

Batting: 30″ × 50″

CUTTING

Exterior fabrics A, B, and C

• Cut a total of 11 strips in any combination as desired:

  Cut 4 strips 3″ × WOF.

  Cut 4 strips 2″ × WOF.

  Cut 3 strips 1″ × WOF.

• From 1 fabric, cut 2 straps 5″ × 34″.

Lining fabric

• Cut 1 rectangle 19″ × 38″.

Backing

• Cut 1 rectangle 23″ × WOF.

Batting

• Cut 2 strips 1½″ × 34″ for straps.

• Cut 1 rectangle 24″ × 41″ for body.

CONSTRUCTION

Seam allowances are ¼˝ unless otherwise noted.

Making the Exterior

Sew the exterior fabric strips together along their long edges as desired or as they appear in the photograph. Press all the seams facing down.

Free-Motion Quilting

1. Baste the exterior with the batting and backing, using your preferred method (see Basting a Quilt, page 34).

2. Attach the darning foot to your sewing machine.

3. Free-motion quilt with an "e" or "l" design or as desired.

4. Once you are finished free-motion quilting, trim the piece to 18˝ × 37˝.

Preparing the Lining

1. To hem the top edge of the pocket, press the one long edge ¼˝ to the wrong side and then another 1˝ to the wrong side. Stitch the hemmed edge in place.

2. Press the remaining 3 sides ½˝ toward the wrong side.

3. Pin the wrong side of the pocket on the right side of the lining fabric with the top edge of the pocket 4˝ down from the top of the lining and one side of the pocket about 5˝ from one side of the lining. Edgestitch all but the top hemmed edge of the pocket to the lining.

4. To create separate sections in the pocket, sew a vertical line of stitching 3˝ from both the right and left sides of the pocket. Make sure to reinforce the stitches on the top and bottom for security. ▶ **FIG.A**

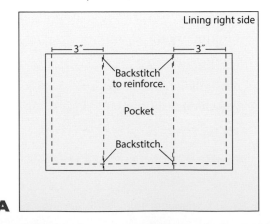

A

Preparing the Straps

1. Press each strap in half with wrong sides together so they measure 2½˝ wide.

2. Open the straps and press the long sides of both straps ¼˝ to wrong side. ▶ **FIG.B**

3. With straps still open, position the narrow strips of batting along the pressed center of each strap. ▶ **FIG.C**

4. Close the straps along the pressed fold with the batting nestled inside and topstitch the layers together, ¼˝ from the long edges of both straps. ▶ **FIG.D**

5. If desired, FMQ the straps with an assortment of e's and l's. Trim the straps to 30˝ long. ▶ **FIG.E**

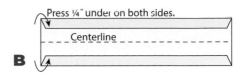

B

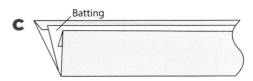

C

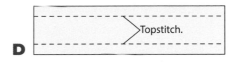

D

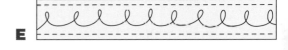

E

Assembling the Tote

1. With the right side of the quilted tote fabric facing up, pin a short end of each strap 4˝ from the right and left side. Keeping the straps flat, measure and pin the opposite end of each strap 13˝ from the right and left sides, as shown. This leaves 7˝ in the center between the 2 straps. ▶ **FIG.F**

F

2. Pin the wrong sides of the exterior and the lining together along the top edge. Make sure the pocket is facing up!

3. Sew a ½˝ seam along the top as pinned, to add strength to the seam. Press this seam toward the lining.

4. Fold the tote in half with the right sides together and raw edges aligned. It will measure approximately 18˝ wide × 36˝ high. Sew the side and bottom edges together in one continuous seam. Leave a 6˝ gap in the stitching on the bottom of the lining so you can turn the tote right side out later. ▶ **FIG.G**

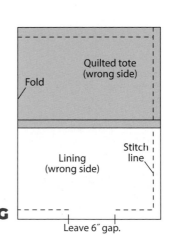

G

5. If desired, box both corners as follows:

a. With wrong sides out, select the seamed corner of the tote exterior and fold it so that the side and bottom seams align.

b. Mark a horizontal line 2˝ up from the corner and sew across. ▶ **FIG.H**

c. Trim off the corner edge ½˝ from the stitching. ▶ **FIG.I**

d. Repeat these steps at the remaining corner of the exterior, approximating where the side seam would be.

e. Repeat these steps to box the 2 bottom corners of the lining.

6. Put your hand through the opening in the bottom seam and hold on to the straps. Use the straps to pull the tote right side out. Sew the opening closed. Press the seam.

7. Place the lining down inside the tote. Topstitch ¼˝ around the top of the tote and on the handles, as desired. Ta–da!! What do you think? You have yourself an awesome homemade tote. ▶ **FIG.J**

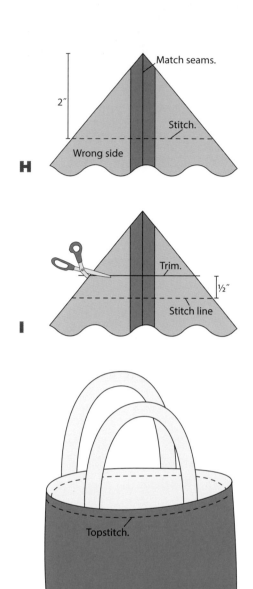

I had so much fun making up the straps for this bag! How about using your new found skills to make a guitar strap or even a belt? The rectangular shape of straps, belts, and all kinds of accessories make the perfect background for e's and l's. I can't wait to see what you come up with—please make sure to tag me when you share your creations on any of your social media sites!

CHAPTER 7

Quilting Loops

WHAT YOU NEED

- Darning foot
- Quilt sandwich, 15″ square

Skills You Learn

- How to use a darning foot
- Stitching on a quilt sandwich
- Moving the three layers of fabric under a needle with a darning foot
- Quilting a design along a prescribed line
- Spacing distance and height
- Creating a design within a design

DESIGN ELEMENTS: LOOPS

Although loops might look like e's and l's there are two very important differences: loops travel don't stay in a straight line and they alternate direction every time they are drawn. I recommend keeping both the shape and size of the loops and the distance between them consistent.

Unlike the e's and l's that travel along a line, loops twist and turn, moving in all directions to fill spaces. One of the main design elements of the loop is the curve that slants inward to form the loop and then reforms when exiting the loop. I like to imagine a nice round bump going into the loop and then the same round bump coming out. These curves, or bumps, ensure a flowing design that is pleasing to the eye.

Learning how to stitch into and out of a loop is critical for the success of this design. Focus on "bumping" into the curve and then "bumping" out for a wonderful overall look to the design.

1. To make a beautiful loop, "bump" into the loop with a nice round curve. ▶ **FIG.A**

2. Keep the line of the loop smooth and gently rounded. ▶ **FIG.B**

3. The curves going in and going out of the loop need to be rounded and like each other. ▶ **FIG.C**

4. Different size loops, the distance between the loops, and the density of the loops help you create a variety of designs. Do, however, keep these factors consistent within a single design. ▶ **FIG.D**

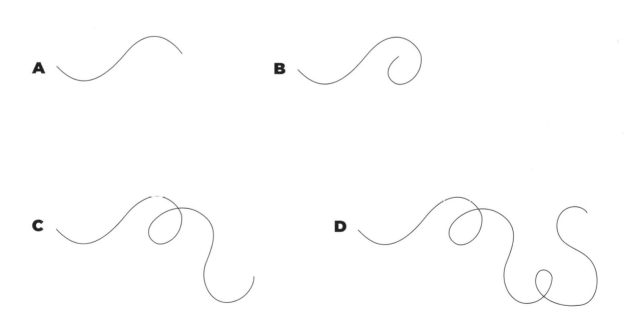

A

B

C

D

Design Variations

Just look at what you can do with these five loop design variations. Which one will you try first?

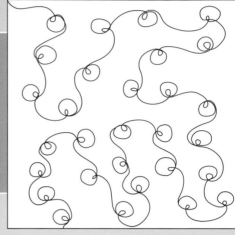

Double Me Up

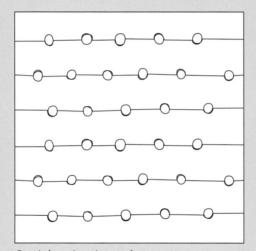

Straightening Around

Mini Buds

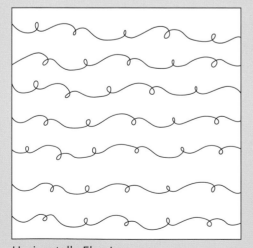

Horizontally Flowing

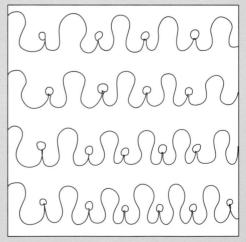

Hills and Vales

Practice Workouts

Date	Time	Task
		Use your finger to trace the loops of all the design variations, starting in the top right corner. Ask yourself what are the design elements? Pay attention to the curves going in and out of the loops.
		On a blank sheet of paper, create loops for 5 minutes.
		Draw 3 boxes approximately 8˝ square. Fill the boxes with loops: the first box with small loops, the second box with medium loops, and the third with larger loops.
		On one sheet of paper, draw loops from bottom to top and then top to bottom for the entire sheet.
		Create the loops with large loops having shorter lines connecting the loops.
		Create small loops on one sheet of paper.
		Vary the size of the loops on another sheet of paper.
		Double up the loops when drawing them.
		Get lined paper and draw loops along the line. Loops can be drawn linear to give a different look. Put the timer on for 5 minutes. Draw all different sizes of loops along the lines on your sheet.
		Get out the quilt sandwich and quilt loops for 5 minutes continuously. Only stop when readjusting your hands.

HEART OF THE HOME
Pillow Cover

Finished pillow cover: 21½˝ × 21½˝

It is so fascinating to understand the historical background of the Log Cabin block. The red center represents the hearth of the home. A yellow center represents a welcoming light in the window. According to folklore, a black center represents a stop for the Underground Railroad. Imagine how much more significance would be attached when making or giving this quilt with this information presented.

MATERIALS AND SUPPLIES

Yardage is based on 44˝-wide fabric.

Red fabric scrap:
For cutting to 3˝ × 3˝ for center

Dark color fabrics:
3 color/print variations

Dark fabric 1: ⅛ yard

Dark fabric 2: ¼ yard

Dark fabric 3: ¼ yard

Light color/white fabrics:
2 color/print variations

Light fabric 1: ⅛ yard

Light fabric 2: ⅛ yard

Pillow cover back: ⅔ yard

Backing: 26˝ × 26˝ for quilted front

Batting: 25˝ × 25˝

Pillow form: 22˝ × 22˝

CUTTING

Red fabric (first section: center square)

- Cut 1 square 3˝ × 3˝.

Dark fabric 1 (second section)

- Cut 1 strip 3˝ × WOF. Subcut:

  1 strip 3˝ × 8˝

  2 strips 3˝ × 5½˝

  1 square 3˝ × 3˝

Light fabric 1 (third section)

- Cut 1 strip 1½˝ × WOF. Subcut:

  1 strip 1½˝ × 10˝

  2 strips 1½˝ × 9˝

  1 strip 1½˝ × 8˝

Dark fabric 2 (fourth section)

- Cut 2 strips 3˝ × WOF. Subcut:

  1 strip 3˝ × 15˝

  2 strips 3˝ × 12½˝

  1 strip 3˝ × 10˝

Light fabric 2 (fifth section)

- Cut 2 strips 1½˝ × WOF. Subcut:

  1 strip 1½˝ × 17˝

  2 strips 1½˝ × 16˝

  1 strip 1½˝ × 15˝

Dark fabric 3 (sixth section: outer border)

- Cut 2 strips 3˝ × WOF. Subcut:

  1 strip 3˝ × 22˝

  2 strips 3˝ × 19½˝

  1 strip 3˝ × 17˝

Pillow cover back

- Cut 1 strip 22˝ × WOF. Subcut:

  1 strip 22˝ × 18˝

  1 strip 22˝ × 15˝

CONSTRUCTION

Seam allowances are ¼˝ unless otherwise noted.
Press all the seams away from the center.

Block Assembly

Refer to the illustration for piecing information.

1. Sew the first section pieces to the center square in the following order:

a. Sew the 3˝ × 3˝ section piece to the center 3˝ × 3˝ square.

b. Sew 1 strip 3˝ × 5½˝ to the newly formed strip.

c. Sew the remaining 3˝ × 5½˝ strip and then the final 3˝ × 8˝ strip in a clockwise direction to form a square. ▶ **FIG.A**

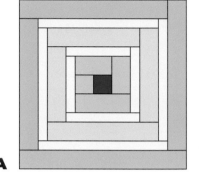

A

2. Continue in the same manner for each section, stitching the shortest strip of each section first, then the 2 medium-length strips, and the longest strip last. Once all the strips are sewn and pressed, the finished pillow cover front should measure 22˝ × 22˝ square.

Free-Motion Quilting

1. Baste the front pillow cover to the backing and batting, using your preferred method (see Basting a Quilt, page 34).

2. Attach the darning foot to your sewing machine.

3. Free-motion quilt with a loop design or as desired. ▶ **FIG.B**

B

Finishing

1. Press and trim the quilted pillow cover front to 22˝ square.

2. Hem one long (22˝) edge of both pillow cover back pieces by pressing ¼˝ to the wrong side and then 1˝. Topstitch along the pressed edges. ▶ **FIG.C**

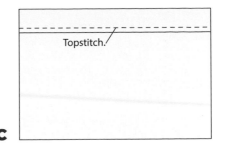

3. Place the pillow front facing up, and with right sides together and raw edges aligned, place the larger back piece down first and then the smaller back piece down, so that the hemmed edges overlap. Pin the pieces together around the outside edges.

4. Stitch around the perimeter of the pillow cover with ½˝ seam allowances.

5. Turn the pillow cover right side out. Insert the pillow form and your Log Cabin pillow cover is ready for accessorizing any bed, couch, or chair!

Log Cabin Quilt

Finished quilt: 68½″ × 91″

With more fabric and more time, you can use the skills you mastered making a Log Cabin pillow cover to make a twelve-block Log Cabin quilt!

MATERIALS AND SUPPLIES

Red fabric: ⅛ yard for centers

Dark fabrics: 3 color/print variations (This assumes that dark fabric 1 and dark fabric 3 are each used for sections 2 and 6 in 6 blocks, and dark fabric 2 is used for section 4 in all 12 blocks.)

  Dark fabric 1: 1½ yards

  Dark fabric 2: 1½ yards

  Dark fabric 3: 1½ yards

Light fabric: 2 color/print variations (This assumes that light fabric 1 is used for section 3, sashing, and outer border, and light fabric 2 is used for section 5.)

  Light fabric 1: 1½ yards

  Light fabric 2: 1⅛ yards

Binding: ¾ yard

Backing: 4½ yards (if pieced with horizontal seam) or 6 yards (if pieced with vertical seam)

Batting: 76″ × 98″

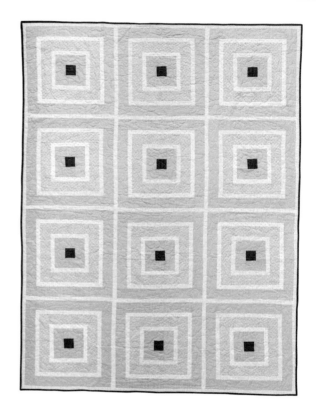

CUTTING

Red fabric (first section: center square)

· Cut 12 squares 3″ × 3″.

Dark fabric 1 (second and sixth sections)

· Cut 16 strips 3″ × WOF. Subcut:

  6 strips 3″ × 22″

  12 strips 3″ × 19½″

  6 strips 3″ × 17″

  6 strips 3″ × 8″

  12 strips 3″ × 5½″

  6 squares 3″ × 3″

Dark fabric 2 (fourth section)

- Cut 12 strips 3″ × WOF. Subcut:

  12 strips 3″ × 15″

  24 strips 3″ × 12½″

  12 strips 3″ × 10″

Dark fabric 3 (second and sixth sections)

- Cut 16 strips 3″ × WOF. Subcut:

  6 strips 3″ × 22″

  12 strips 3″ × 19½″

  6 strips 3″ × 17″

  6 strips 3″ × 8″

  12 strips 3″ × 5½″

  6 squares 3″ × 3″

Light fabric 1 (third section, sashing, and outer border)

- Cut 12 strips 1½″ × WOF for third section. Subcut:

  12 strips 1½″ × 10″

  24 strips 1½″ × 9″

  12 strips 1½″ × 8″

- Cut 8 strips 1½″ × WOF for outer border.

- Cut 5 strips 1½″ × WOF for horizontal sashing.

- Cut 5 strips 1½″ × WOF for vertical sashing.

Light fabric 2 (fifth section)

- Cut 24 strips 1½″ × WOF. Subcut:

  12 strips 1½″ × 17″

  24 strips 1½″ × 16″

  12 strips 1½″ × 15″

INSTRUCTIONS

This quilt is made from 12 blocks 21½″ × 21½″, put together exactly like the pillow cover front.

Sew 5 strips 1½″ × WOF together end to end, and then subcut 8 strips 1½″ × 22″ for the vertical sashing.

Sew 5 strips 1½″ × WOF together end to end, and then subcut 3 strips 1½″ × 67″ for the horizontal sashing.

Sew 8 strips 1½″ × WOF together end to end and then subcut 2 strips 1½″ × 69″ for the top and bottom borders and 2 strips 1½″ × 89½″ for the side borders.

Sew the blocks together in 4 rows of 3 with the vertical sashing strips between the blocks.

Then sew the rows together with the horizontal sashing strips between the rows. Add the side border strips and then the top and bottom border strips to the perimeter of the pieced quilt top. Baste the quilt, FMQ the layers, and then bind the edges.

CHAPTER 8

Quilting Daisies

WHAT YOU NEED

- Darning foot
- Quilt sandwich, 15˝ square
- Fabric marking pen or tailor's chalk

Skills You Learn

- How to use a darning foot
- Stitching on a quilt sandwich
- Moving the three layers of fabric under a needle with a darning foot
- Spacing distance and height
- Mirroring a design
- Creating a design within a design

DESIGN ELEMENT: DAISIES

How often do you catch yourself doodling while talking on the phone or watching TV? Drawing daisies was one of my go-to doodles when I was young and I really enjoy quilting them on so many projects.

One of the key aspects of drawing and stitching a daisy correctly is to form a "sharp" center; clean lines in the center make such a difference in the overall look of the flower. The shape of the petal is also important, as well as consistent spacing between petals. If you have an even number of petals, make sure they are symmetrical. If you have an odd number of petals, make sure that they are a mirror image of each other. Symmetry is important for a nice clean look.

So, make a call to a friend you have not talked to for a while, grab your sketch book and favorite pen, and practice, practice, practice.

1. Draw a single petal with equal length and symmetrical sides. ▶ **FIG.A**

2. Decide before you start drawing or stitching the daisy how many petals you want. If you want an even number of petals, make sure the petals are arranged symmetrically. If you were to cut the daisy in half, both sides should be mirror images of each other. No matter how large or how small, the petals should be consistent. ▶ **FIG.B**

3. Draw a second petal. ▶ **FIG.C**

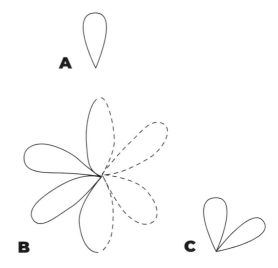

A

B

C

▶ **DARA'S TIP** *If you plan to have an odd number of petals, they should be mirror images in shape and size.*

4. Make sure the petals are consistent sizes. Draw so all the petal ends meet at the same point—in the center. Or if the daisy has a circular center, make sure the lines of the petals touch the circle and do not cross over it. ▶ **FIG.D**

5. Join multiple daisies with a "joining line." The length of the line between daisies can vary or remain consistent. In this example, all the joining lines are about ½˝ long. Try not to let the joining line dissect the petals; be aware of the petal locations. ▶ **FIG.E**

6. Play with the joining lines by stitching e's between the daisies. ▶ **FIG.F**

▶ **DARA'S TIP** *When my needle hits the center of the joining flower, I make a mental note that I made the connection, I pause for just a moment to assure the connection, and then I continue stitching.*

D

E

F

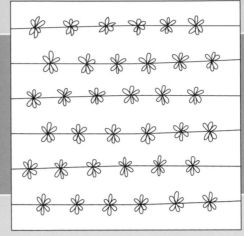

Daisy on the Line

Design Variations

Here are five other daisy design variations. Which one will you try first?

Circle Daisy

Windmills

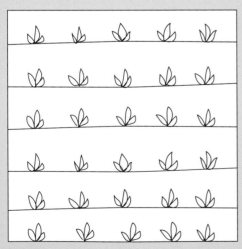

Lotus

Double Daisy

Practice Workouts

Date	Time	Task
		With a lined piece of paper, draw one row of 5 petal daisies side by side, not joined. Draw the daisies about 1˝ in size. Now draw another row of daisies the same size and join them. How did you join them without raising your pen?
		Set your timer for 5 minutes. Draw as many different types of daisies as you can think of.
		Draw 5-petal, 6-petal, 7-petal, and 8-petal daisies for the next 5 minutes. What feels most comfortable to draw? What looks the best? Do you like the symmetry of the even petals?
		Set the timer for another 5 minutes, and draw all your daisies focusing on making the petals all the same size and shape.
		Have you ever heard of a double daisy? It is a petal within a petal. Draw double daisies for the next 5 minutes. Daisies are typically between 1˝ and 2˝ across.
		Now try to create triple daisies drawn in a variety of sizes.
		Take a blank piece of paper and fold it into quadrants. In the top left quadrant, draw a connected series of daisies until it is filled. Move to the top right quadrant and continue to draw daisies. Move down to the bottom right and draw until that space is filled. Finally, complete the page by drawing daisies in the bottom left quadrant.
		Complete the same exercise that you completed with pen and paper in workout #7 but with thread and the quilt sandwich.
		Stitch an 8˝ square on your quilt sandwich and fill the space with a combination of single, double, and triple daisies. Then take a picture and share it with me or share it on your social media and tag me in your picture so I can celebrate your progress!

HE LOVES ME, HE LOVES ME NOT
Apron

TWO SIZES!

Finished apron:

Adult size: Approximately 32″ × 36″

Child/Small adult size: Approximately 23″ × 32″

So many relationships are formed around a table eating food. Now that all five of my kids are at school all day, I look forward to being together at mealtime. This project includes cutting instructions for two apron sizes: one for kids or small adults and one for adults. Feel free to customize these (and all) aprons—change the fabric; piece it as you prefer; add ruffles on pockets, straps, or hems; or even add appliqué initials. I have made aprons as gifts, sold aprons at craft sales, made many special-order aprons, and even made aprons as party favors for my daughter's cupcake birthday party. Once again, let your imagination take over and cook up some yummy variations.

NOTE: Apron Fabrics

Here are some thoughts on how to select the best fabric for all-occasion aprons.

· What is the purpose of the apron? Will you use it every day?

· Where will you store your apron? Do you have a hook for it in your kitchen?

· Will it become a kitchen accessory?

· Will it be seasonal or suitable for all seasons?

· Who is the apron for? Are they sports fans? Do they love a specific thing such as apples?

· Does everyone in the family have their own apron?

· Do you plan to quilt the fabric and will it be worn by different people of different sizes?

MATERIALS AND SUPPLIES

Yardage is based on 44˝-wide fabric.

ADULT APRON

Fabric 1: ⅜ yard

Fabric 2: ⅜ yard

Fabric 3: ⅜ yard

Fabric 4: ¾ yard for waist ties, neck straps, and binding

Backing: 1⅛ yards

Batting: 40˝ × 44˝

CHILD/SMALL ADULT APRON

Fabric 1: ⅜ yard

Fabric 2: ⅜ yard

Fabric 3: ⅜ yard

Fabric 4: ¾ yard for waist ties, neck straps, and binding

Backing: 1 yard

Batting: 31˝ × 40˝

CUTTING

ADULT APRON

- **Fabric 1:** Cut 2 strips 5˝ × WOF. Subcut 5˝ squares. You need 16.

- **Fabric 2:** Cut 2 strips 5˝ × WOF. Subcut 5˝ squares. You need 16.

- **Fabric 3:** Cut 2 strips 5˝ × WOF. Subcut 5˝ squares. You need 14.

- **Fabric 4:**

  Cut 3 strips 5˝ × WOF: 1 strip for neck straps and 2 strips for waist ties.

  Cut 4 strips 2½˝ × WOF for binding.

CHILD/SMALL ADULT APRON

- **Fabric 1:** Cut 2 strips 5˝ × WOF. Subcut 5˝ squares. You need 11.

- **Fabric 2:** Cut 2 strips 5˝ × WOF. Subcut 5˝ squares. You need 10.

- **Fabric 3:** Cut 2 strips 5˝ × WOF. Subcut 5˝ squares. You need 10.

- **Fabric 4:**

  Cut 3 strips 5˝ × WOF: 1 strip for neck straps and 2 strips for waist ties.

  Cut 3 strips 2½˝ × WOF for binding.

CONSTRUCTION

Seam allowances are ¼˝ unless otherwise noted.

Piecing the Apron Front

1. Refer to the diagram to lay out the squares in the sequences as indicated. There are two different layouts: one for an adult apron and one for a small adult or child apron.

For adult apron:

▶ **FIG.A**

Fabric 1: 16 squares

Fabric 2: 16 squares

Fabric 3: 14 squares

For child/small adult apron:

▶ **FIG.B**

Fabric 1: 11 squares

Fabric 2: 10 squares

Fabric 3: 10 squares

2. Sew all the horizontal rows one at a time. After all the rows are sewn, press the seam allowances for the odd rows to the right and the even rows to the left.

3. Sew the rows to each other. Press all the seams toward the bottom of the apron. The apron is now ready to be basted and free-motion quilted using the daisy design.

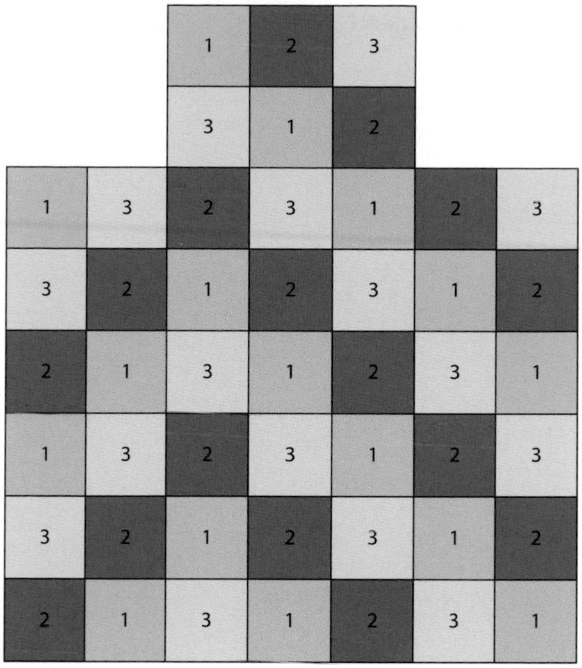

A

Adult apron layout

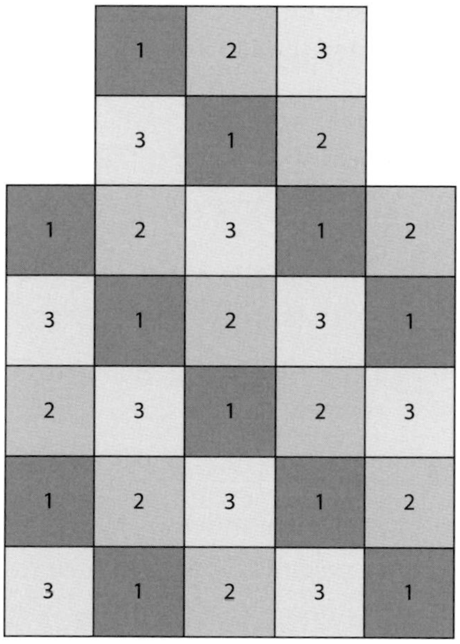

B

Child/small adult apron layout

Free-Motion Quilting

1. Baste the apron top to the batting and backing with your preferred method (see Basting a Quilt, page 34).

2. Attach the darning foot.

3. I purposefully designed this project to provide a grid for FMQ a daisy in each square. As always, feel free to use your own daisy design or any design inside and outside the pieced squares. You might want to try quilting 3 smaller daisies in each square! ▶ **FIG.C**

4. Trim the batting and backing even with the quilt top's edges after you finish quilting.

▶ **DARA'S TIP** *Professional quilters often use the piecing of a quilt to organize their free-motion quilting, especially when custom quilting.*

Preparing the Neck Straps and Waist Ties

1. Cut the neck strap into 2 pieces, one 22″ long and the other 6½″ long. Discard the rest of the strap or save it for future projects.

2. Fold the neck straps and waist ties in half lengthwise with right sides together. Stitch the long edge and one short edge. Reinforce the beginning and end stitches and trim the stitched corner diagonally to reduce bulk. ▶ **FIG.D**

3. Turn the straps and ties right side out. Use a blunt pair of scissors or a chopstick to square up the corners. Press.

4. Topstitch along the 3 closed edges, as indicated. Press. Put the straps and ties aside while you shape and prepare the apron body. ▶ **FIG.E**

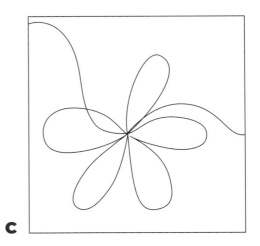

C

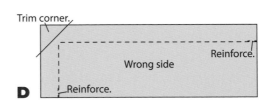

Trim corner.

Reinforce.

Wrong side

D Reinforce.

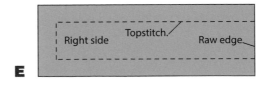

Right side   Topstitch.   Raw edge.

E

Finishing

1. Shape the apron sides. Draw the desired shape of the apron sides freehand or trace the shape of an existing apron or even a curved platter on one side of the quilted piece. To assure that the shape of the apron sides is identical, fold the piece in half lengthwise and trace the drawn curved edge on the opposite side. Cut along the marked lines. ▶ **FIG.F**

2. Make the binding (see Making and Attaching Binding, page 37).

3. Fold the shorter neck strap in half and press. Pin both neck straps to the right side of the apron, raw edges aligned and ¾˝ from the sides, as shown. Baste them in place. ▶ **FIG.G**

4. Pin the right side of the binding to the wrong side of all the apron edges with raw edges aligned.

5. Sew the binding to the apron, catching the neck straps in the stitching. Fold the binding to the right side and stitch by hand or machine to enclose the raw edges.

6. Once the binding is attached extend the straps away from the apron and, from the back, stitch along the edge of the binding one more time to secure the straps in place. ▶ **FIG.H**

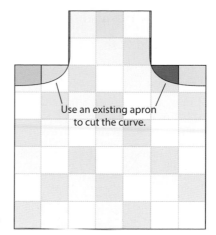

Use an existing apron to cut the curve.

F

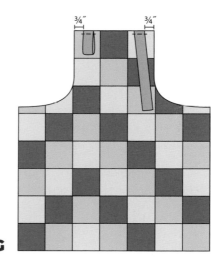

¾˝   ¾˝

G

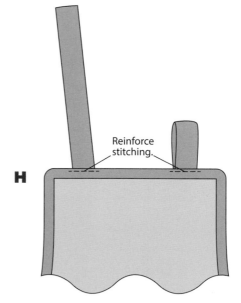

Reinforce stitching.

H

7. Hold or pin the apron on the recipient to determine where to position the waist ties. They usually are positioned just below where the curve ends. Mark the placement on the back of the apron, an inch in from the edges.

8. Fold the raw edge of each waist tie ¾˝ over to the wrong side. Pin the folded edge to the wrong side of the apron at the marking. Stitch the folded ends of the ties to the apron forming a rectangle the width of the ties and about 1½˝ deep. After stitching the rectangles, stitch an X through the center of the rectangular stitching to reinforce.

9. Tie the long neck strap through the short loop to wear the apron. Bon appétit!

Quick and Yummy Quilt

Finished quilt: 50″ × 50″

A fast and fun quilt project using the same easy-peasy design that we used for the aprons. Can't you just imagine snuggling in this quilt while you eat those delicious cookies you just baked in your coordinating apron—how very domestic of you! Way to go!

Follow the same instructions as for the apron, only on a slightly larger scale! Try your hand at this simple quilt.

MATERIALS AND SUPPLIES

Fabric A: ¾ yard

Fabric B: ¾ yard

Fabric C: ¾ yard

Binding: ½ yard

Backing: 3¼ yards

Batting: 58″ × 58″

INSTRUCTIONS

From each of Fabric A, B, and C, cut 5 strips 5″ × WOF.

Strip piece one of each of the 3 fabrics to make 4 sets and then subcut each set into 5″ units. Subcut the remaining single strips into 5″ squares too.

Lay out the strip units as desired, filling in with the single squares. Stitch the rows together, quilt as desired, and attach the binding.

CHAPTER 9

Quilting Paisleys

WHAT YOU NEED

- Darning foot
- Quilt sandwich, 15″ square
- Rotary cutter
- Quilting ruler, 2″ wide
- Fabric marking pen

Skills You Learn

- How to use a darning foot
- Stitching on a quilt sandwich
- Moving the three layers of fabric under a needle with a darning foot
- Quilting a design along a prescribed line
- Echo stitching around the design
- Creating a design within a design

DESIGN ELEMENT: PAISLEYS

The paisley design was one of the first stitches I learned that helped me feel confident as I quilted in multiple directions. The design looks complicated and beautiful but it is relatively easy to stitch with successful and satisfying results. The paisley is basically a transformed teardrop or raindrop and it can be simply echoed, pivoted, and then repeated in different directions for vastly different effects.

When I first watched videos of people free-motion quilting, I often panicked because I could not understand how they knew where to go next. The paisley design seems to effortlessly open and create pathways for the next possibility. See the step-by-steps for a quick easy start to FMQ paisleys.

1. Draw a raindrop (or paisley). Keep the point distinct and crisp. ▶ **FIG.A**

2. Draw another raindrop beside the first raindrop so the pointed ends are together. Note how the design tapers in at the bottom. ▶ **FIG.B**

3. This is where the design gets interesting because you can "grow" the design by drawing the next raindrop, or paisley, in the "valley" between the two existing designs. New growth occurs between a pair of two raindrops/paisleys. ▶ **FIG.C**

▶ **DARA'S TIP** *Words have great meaning. If your version of the paisley shape looks more like a petal or a teardrop, call it that—having the design make sense to you is important.*

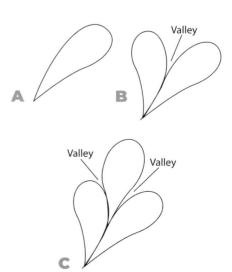

4. Watch how the design grows as you continue to add paisleys. Something to keep in mind with this design is that you can get to where you want to go by echoing the shape. ▶ **FIG.D**

5. Just look at the progression of this design. ▶ **FIG.E**

▶ **DARA'S TIP**

Sometimes, if you find your quilting squished in a corner, simply create half of the design and use the border or edge of your quilt to travel along.

Free-Motion Quilting Terminology

Here are a few FMQ terms to add to your repertoire.

Echo The process of repeating the same shape and pattern within a close parallel or repetition. The echoing of most designs does not need to retain the same width all the way around.

Pivot The pivot point is the central point on which the design turns or changes direction. Stitch the first paisley and then repeat the design by starting the second paisley at an angle from the beginning or ending of the first paisley. Continue!

Travel stitching Allows you to stitch anywhere within the body of the quilt; it gets you where you want to go. Stitching-in-the-ditch, stitching along the edge of a quilt, or stitching over existing stitched lines are all different ways of travel stitching. Think of it like bold text to provide emphasis, use travel stitching to create emphasis.

Design Variations

Just look at what you can do with these five paisley design variations. Which one will you try first?

Cornucopia

Sprout

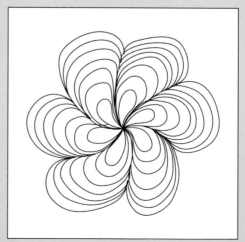

Double Up

Ruffle

Swirl

Practice Workouts

Date	Time	Task
		On a blank piece of paper, draw a raindrop, but create a bend in it. Do this for 3 minutes.
		Echo the bent raindrop 4 times. Repeat 5 more times.
		Draw 2 paisley drops, side by side, without lifting the pen and then add a third paisley between the first two. Can you see where else to add another paisley?
		Fold a blank piece of paper into quadrants. In the top left corner, fill up the space growing raindrops from previous raindrops, never lifting your pen.
		In the top right corner, draw extra-large paisleys.
		In the bottom left corner, draw small paisleys
		In the bottom right corner, echo twice per paisley and then change direction.
		Start at the bottom of a page and with 2 back-and-forth paisley "teardrops," work your way up the paper, drawing them in a zigzag style. What do you notice about the shapes of the tears?
		Can you think of another way to draw paisleys? Doodle one different variation.
		Set the timer for 5 minutes and start drawing paisleys. Do not lift the pen until the timer goes off. How much "ground" did you cover? How does your hand feel?

OHIO STAR
Table Runner

Finished table runner: 18˝ × 38˝

Want to try a new block but don't want to make an entire quilt? This table runner is the perfect solution. The Ohio Star block is a classic design that includes some new techniques. If you've made three blocks and want more, there's a bonus project for you at the end of this project.

MATERIALS AND SUPPLIES

Yardage is based on 44˝–wide fabric.

Print/contrast fabrics: 3 different scraps, each larger than 4˝ square, for center squares

Fabric A: ¾ yard for Hourglass blocks, sashing, and borders

Fabric B: ¼ yard for Hourglass blocks

Binding: ⅜ yard

Backing: 1⅜ yards

Batting: 24˝ × 45˝

CUTTING

Print/contrast fabrics

· From each of the 3 scraps,
  cut 1 square 4˝ × 4˝.

Fabric A

· Cut 1 strip 5˝ × WOF. Subcut 6 squares
  5˝ × 5˝; then cut 2 squares 4˝ × 4˝.

· Cut 1 strip 4˝ × WOF.
  Subcut 10 squares 4˝ × 4˝.

· Cut 2 strips 4˝ × WOF.
  Subcut 2 border strips 4˝ × 38˝.

· Cut 2 strips 2˝ × WOF.
  Subcut 4 sashing strips 2˝ × 11˝.

Fabric B

· Cut 1 strip 5˝ × WOF.
  Subcut 6 squares 5˝ × 5˝.

Backing fabric

· Cut 1 rectangle 24˝ × 47˝
  (cut lengthwise).

Binding

· Cut 4 strips 2½˝ × WOF.

CONSTRUCTION

Seam allowances are ¼˝ unless otherwise noted.

Making Center Blocks

Make 12 Hourglass blocks to complete 3 center blocks.

1. Draw a 45° line on the back of a fabric A 5˝ square.
▶ **FIG.A**

2. Pin a 5˝ fabric B square to a marked fabric A 5˝ square with right sides together; stitch ¼˝ away from both sides of the marked line. ▶ **FIG.B**

3. Cut along the marked line and press each section toward the darker fabric. You now have 2 half-square triangles (HST). ▶ **FIG.C**

4. Place two HST together with the right sides together and rotate the top HST so that the fabrics are opposite and the seams "nest." Draw another 45° line on one of the HST bisecting the seam. Stitch ¼˝ away from both sides of the marked line. ▶ **FIG.D**

5. Cut along the marked line and press. You now have 2 Hourglass blocks. Square up the Hourglass blocks so they are 4˝ square, with the seam intersection exactly in the center. This is an important step, so it helps to use a 4˝-wide quilting ruler and rotary cutter.

6. Repeat Steps 1–5 to make 12 Hourglass blocks.
▶ **FIG.E**

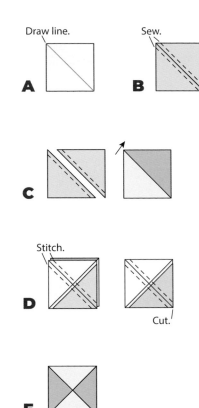

Assembling the Top

1. Lay out 4 Hourglass blocks, 4 fabric A 4˝ squares, and 1 center contrast fabric square in the Ohio Star configuration, as shown. Make sure the Hourglass blocks are all oriented correctly. Sew row by row. Press the seam allowances for the top and bottom rows outward and the middle row inward. The block will measure 11˝ square including seam allowances. Repeat two more times. ▶ **FIG.F**

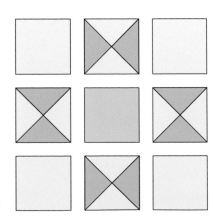

2. Lay out the top of the table runner as shown, with the blocks in the desired sequence. With right sides together, sew a 2″ × 11″ sashing strip between the blocks and to each end of the joined blocks. Press seam allowances toward the sashing strips.

3. With right sides together, sew the border strips to the long edges of the table runner. Press the seam allowances toward the outside. ▶ FIG.G

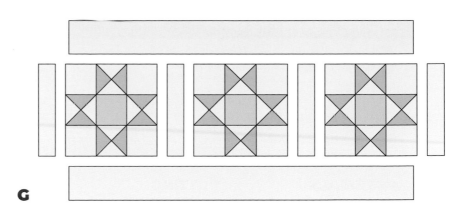

G

Free-Motion Quilting

1. Baste the table runner to the backing and batting with your preferred method (see Basting a Quilt, page 34).

2. Attach the darning foot, and go for it! Enjoy your free-motion quilting. ▶ FIG.H

H

Finishing

1. Trim the table runner with a rotary cutter and long ruler so the edges are even.

2. Make and attach the binding (see Making and Attaching Binding, page 37).

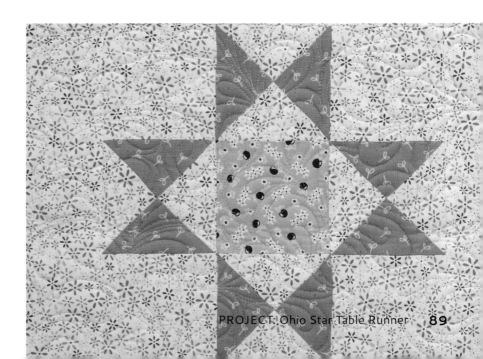

Ohio Star Quilt

Finished quilt: 70˝ × 70½˝

Want something larger than a table runner? Make this quilt—a larger scale and with the opportunity to show more variations in the Hourglass blocks!

MATERIALS AND SUPPLIES

Yardage is based on 44˝-wide fabric.

Fabric A: ⅜ yard or 25 scraps at least 4˝ × 4˝ for center blocks

Fabric B: 4 yards for Hourglass blocks, sashing, and borders

Fabric C: 1¼ yards for Hourglass blocks

Binding: ⅝ yard

Backing: 4 yards

Batting: 79˝ × 79˝

CUTTING

Fabric A

- Cut 25 squares 4˝ × 4˝.

Fabric B

- Cut 7 strips 5˝ × WOF. Subcut 50 squares 5˝ × 5˝.
- Cut 10 strips 4˝ × WOF. Subcut 100 squares 4˝ × 4˝.
- Cut 6 strips 4˝ × WOF and sew them end to end. Subcut 4 horizontal sashing strips 4˝ × 67˝.
- Cut 7 strips 2˝ × WOF. Subcut 20 vertical sashing strips 2˝ × 11˝.
- Cut 7 strips 2½˝ × WOF and sew them end to end. Subcut:
  2 strips 2½˝ × 71˝ for side borders
  2 strips 2½˝ × 67˝ for top and bottom borders

Fabric C

- Cut 7 strips 5˝ × WOF. Subcut 50 squares 5˝ × 5˝.

Backing fabric

- Cut 2 rectangles 72˝ × WOF; sew together lengthwise.

Binding

- Cut 8 strips 2½˝ × WOF.

INSTRUCTIONS

Follow the same construction steps as for the Ohio Star Table Runner (page 86), but make 25 Ohio Star blocks, and set them in 5 rows of 5 stars with vertical sashing strips between the blocks. Sew the rows together with horizontal sashing strips in between; then add the outer borders.

Quilt assembly

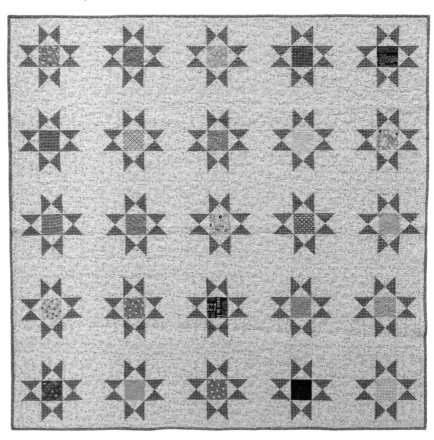

CHAPTER 10

Quilting Stipple, Meandering, and Puzzle Designs

WHAT YOU NEED

- Darning foot
- Quilt sandwich, 15˝ square
- Quilting ruler
- Fabric marking pen

Skills You Learn

- How to use a darning foot
- Stitching on a quilt sandwich
- Moving the three layers of fabric under a needle with a darning foot
- Quilting a design along a prescribed line
- Spacing distance and height
- Mirroring a design
- Creating a design within a design

DESIGN ELEMENTS: STIPPLING, MEANDERING, AND PUZZLES

When I first started teaching free-motion quilting I started with stippling and meandering designs, which were a bit frustrating for some of my students because of the practice needed to create flowing lines and a sense of movement. There are three important design elements: nice round curves (I like to say bump in and bump out), using the curves, or bumps, to fill in space, and having a travel plan for where you want your stitches to go.

1. It is important to "bump" into the curve.
▶ **FIG.A**

2. It is equally important to "bump" out of the curve. ▶ **FIG.B**

3. Turn the design by elongating the length of the bump and the curve. ▶ **FIG.C**

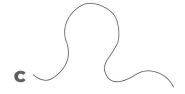

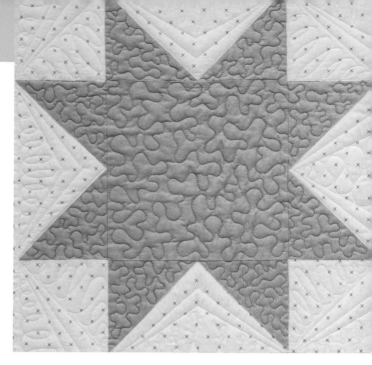

4. Add different size bumps and curves to fill space. This design can be quilted in all different scales. The most important part is to keep the spacing consistent to reduce holes or gaps in the stitching which can be very visible. ▶ **FIG.D**

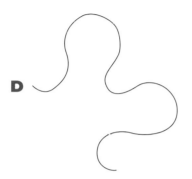

D

▶ **DARA'S TIP** If you fail to plan, you plan to fail. *I find it helpful to use my finger to trace where I am going to go before putting needle and thread into the fabric. This helps increase the flow of the quilting and increases confidence in the action plan.*

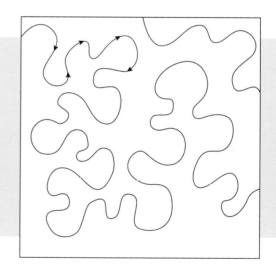

Design Variations

Just look at what you can do with these five meandering and stippling design variations. Which one will you try first?

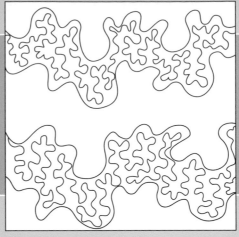

Stipple within a Stipple

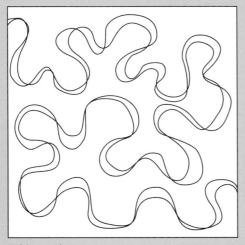

Ribbon Chase

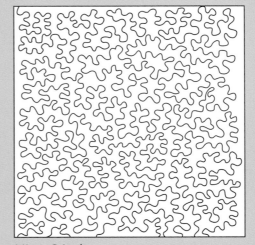

Micro Stipple

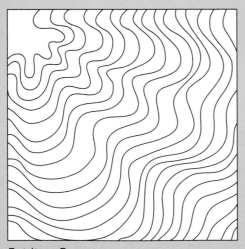

Put It on Repeat

Horizontal Plane

Practice Workouts

Date	Time	Task
		Trace your finger around the various examples provided. Name three things you notice about the designs?
		On a blank piece of paper, recreate a meandering or stipple design. Set the timer for 5 minutes. What do you notice now about the design? What are the differences between your design and those in the book? What do you like about your drawing? What could you do differently?
		On a blank piece of paper, start at the top left corner and draw 3 "bumps" in a row and then change directions. Continue to do so as you make your way around the piece of paper. Fill the paper.
		Fold a blank piece of paper into quarters. In the top left corner, draw the meandering/stippling in a medium scale. Fill the space as evenly as you can.
		In the top right corner, draw the meandering/stippling in a large scale. Fill the space as evenly as you can.
		In the bottom right corner, draw the meandering/stippling in a small scale. Fill the space as evenly as you can.
		In the bottom left corner, draw the meandering/stippling in a micro scale. Fill the space as evenly as you can.
		Draw a 4″ square. Draw a 6″ square around the smaller square and then an 8″ square around the medium square. In the center square, stipple in a small scale. In the border of the medium square, stipple at a medium scale. In the last outside border, stipple with the small scale again. Do not lift the pen when transitioning from one border to another.
		Quilting yourself out of a corner can be tricky. Draw a 4″ square and meander inside the box; when you hit an edge, stop and trace down the line, and then continue back along the same design within the box.
		Stitch over a quilt sandwich that is already heavily quilted. Change the thread color and then meander around all the previously stitched designs. Note how versatile this is for an allover design.

SO HAPPY TOGETHER
Place Mats

Finished place mat: 15˝ × 18˝

I can't think of a celebration that doesn't involve food. Can you? I enjoy having a beautifully laid out table to complement the food that I have made because it makes the occasion more special. My sister-in-law gifted me six red quilted place mats for my birthday. They are one of my all-time favorite gifts. They are practical, pretty, and add color and pizazz to our meals. Quite often when my family sits down to eat, we think of Aunt Kellee and our fun times with cousins and extended family.

Fabric Considerations and Selection

FABRIC CONSIDERATIONS

· Do you have children at your table? If young children will be using the place mats, you might want to choose darker colors and busy prints to hide stains. And use 100% cotton fabric to hide stains well.

· Do you want to match your kitchen decor?

· Where will the place mats be stored? Will they be displayed in a basket on the table or tucked away?

· Do you want to be able to use both sides of the place mat? If they are going to be seasonal designs, you might want to make one side for Valentine's Day and the other for Thanksgiving, for instance.

· Since place mats require frequent washing, avoid shrinkage by prewashing the fabric before piecing and quilting the place mats.

· Color choice affects the mood of a meal; bright colors evoke energy and joy, light colors can be subtle and calming, while traditional colors such as navy and forest green are more conservative.

FABRIC SELECTION

· This is your project and it's important that you like the finished place mats.

· Gather fabrics that you like and group them together. Leave them for a bit and come back to them several times to reassess. Do you still like them every time you look? Are any of the fabrics distracting? Take away fabrics that aren't appealing and add different fabrics until you love the combination.

· Take a picture of the fabrics with a digital camera and turn the picture into gray-scale to check the balance of values of the fabrics.

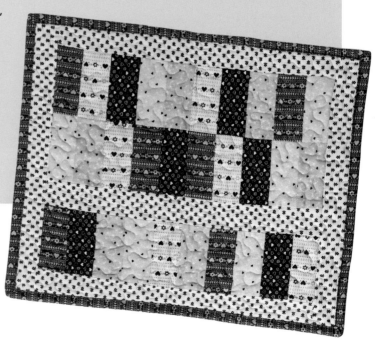

MATERIALS AND SUPPLIES

Yardage is based on 44˝-wide fabric and is enough to make 4 place mats.

Main fabrics: 5 fat quarters (A–E)

Sashing and border fabric: ⅝ yard

Binding: ⅔ yard

Backing: 1 yard

Batting: 24˝ × 96˝ *or* 44˝ × 48˝ (You can cut the batting for the 4 mats either from a long strip or in a 2–across format from a wider rectangle.)

CUTTING

Fat quarters A–E

- From *each* fat quarter, cut 5 strips 2˝ × 22˝.

Sashing and border

- Cut 10 strips 2˝ × WOF. Subcut into 20 strips 2˝ × 15½˝.

Binding

- Cut 8 strips 2½˝ × WOF.

CONSTRUCTION

Seam allowances are ¼˝ unless otherwise noted. Press the seams open and flat.

Making the Place Mat Tops

1. Keep the strips cut from the fat quarters in 5 separate groups (A, B, C, D, and E).

▶ **DARA'S TIP** *I recommend labeling each fabric with a designated letter to help keep track.*

2. Sew the strips into the sets in this order:

Strip set #1: A, C, B, E, D

Strip set #2: C, B, D, A, E

Strip set #3: B, E, A, D, C

Strip set #4: C, D, E, B, A

Strip set #5: A, B, C, D, E

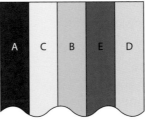

Strip set #1

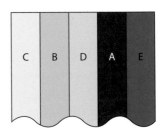

Strip set #2

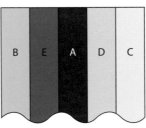

Strip set #3

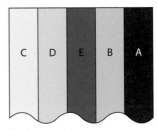

Strip set #4

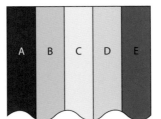

Strip set #5

Press the seams open to keep the place mats as flat as possible and so plates and cups don't wobble!

3. Subcut all the strip sets into rectangles 4″ × 8″. Each strip set yields 5 pieces. Keep the sets together.

4. Stitch the sets together in pairs along a short edge as follows:

Place mat #1:

Set 1 with set 4

Set 2 with set 5

Set 3 with set 1

Place mat #2:

Set 2 with set 5

Set 3 with set 1

Set 4 with set 2

Place mat #3:

Set 3 with set 1

Set 4 with set 2

Set 5 with set 3

Place mat #4:

Set 4 with set 2

Set 5 with set 3

Set 1 with set 4

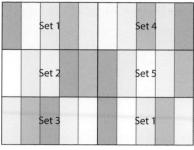

Place mat #1

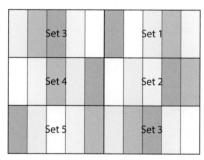

Place mat #2

Place mat #3

Place mat #4

5. To assemble the place mat, stitch the first two paired strip sets together along the long edges with right sides together. Line up the seams for a nice crisp finish. Press and trim to 7½″ × 15½″. Sew a sashing strip to the bottom edge of this unit. Then sew the remaining long edge of the sashing strip to the top edge of the remaining set.

6. Sew border strips to the bottom and the top edges. Press and then add the two side borders (2″ × 15½″). ▶ FIG. A

A

Free-Motion Quilting

1. Baste the place mats to backing and batting with your preferred method (see Basting a Quilt, page 34).

2. Attach the darning foot.

3. Free-motion quilt with a meandering design or as desired.

Finishing

1. Press and trim the place mats to 15½″ × 18″.

2. Prepare and attach the binding (see Making and Attaching Binding, page 37).

Bon appétit!

INSTRUCTIONS

Customize these or any place mats for family members with an appliquéd letter for their first name. Or maybe add an appliqué of a favorite object like a basketball. My kids thought it would be funny to put SG on one for "Special Guest."

It is easy to cut letters and shapes from felt, spray baste them in place, and then FMQ!

And while you are at it, use a slow cooker to prepare your dinner so you can spend time sewing rather than cooking. Perhaps we can swap a favorite recipe!

CHAPTER 11

Quilting Circuit Boards

Skills You Learn

- How to use a darning foot
- Stitching on a quilt sandwich
- Moving the three layers of fabric under a needle with a darning foot
- Quilting a design along a prescribed line
- Spacing distance and height
- Mirroring a design
- Creating a design within a design

WHAT YOU NEED

- Darning foot
- Quilt sandwich, 15˝ square

DESIGN ELEMENT: CIRCUIT BOARDS

This linear design does not require a ruler and it is a great way to become more comfortable with travelling your stitches in a variety of directions. I have a very simple trick to help you master this design. Imagine that you are drawing with an Etch A Sketch. The only way to travel is to turn the knobs. You simply ask yourself: *Which way do I want to go? Left? Right? Up? Down?*

A circuit board design features squares and rectangles of all shapes and sizes that intersect each other. The amount of space between designs can be varied; however, the spacing should be kept relatively consistent to avoid "holes" in the quilting. Rule of thumb: cross the line that you just created.

1. Draw a line up or down then stop. If it helps you know how long to draw the line, count to two, then stop. Turn left or right. Again, count to two. If you desire longer lines, count longer. If you desire shorter lines, count to one. ▶ **FIG.A**

2. Repeat the same process moving up and down or left to right along the quilted surface. If you need to stop, keep the needle in the down position and stop at one of the intersections. ▶ **FIG.B**

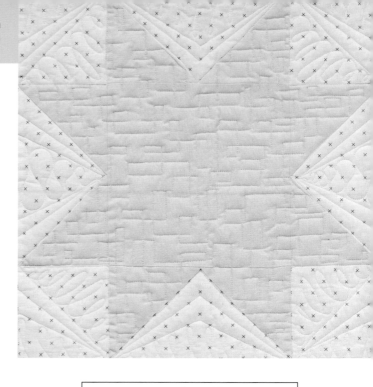

3. Continue stitching, turning always with right angles. ▶ **FIG.C**

4. Continue the path of creating new rectangles and squares. I encourage you to trace the path in this illustration with your finger to develop your muscle memory. ▶ **FIG.D**

5. There are so many the possible quilting progressions using this design. ▶ **FIGS.E–G**

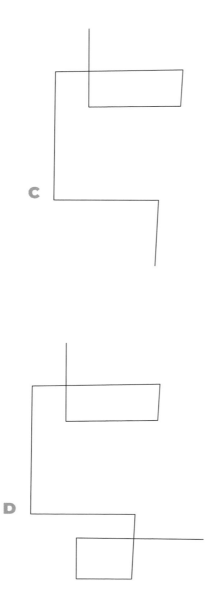

C

D

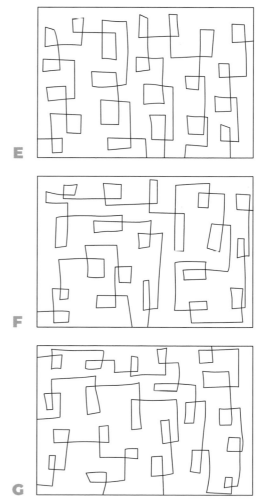

E

F

G

Design Variations

Here are five other circuit board variations. Which one will you try first?

Connected

Reverberate

Electronic Crabs

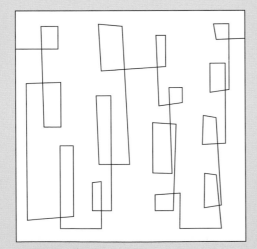

Long Way Home

Dare to Be Square

Practice Workouts

Date	Time	Task
		On a lined piece of paper, put your pen down on the top left line and draw continuous boxes all the way across the paper, not lifting the pen and only filling up one line. When you have reached the end of the line, move the pen down and continue drawing on the next row from right to left. Do this for 5 minutes.
		Do the same workout as indicated previously, but change the size so the boxes are three rows wide. It is important to change the scale of these designs. Continue this for 5 minutes. Make sure the corners are as close to a 90° angle as you can make them.
		Trace your finger on one of the circuit board samples found in the book. What do you notice about the design? How would you explain how to create this design to a fellow quilter?
		On a lined piece of paper and with a timer set for 5 minutes, try to recreate a circuit design. Fill the space without lifting the pen. The goal is to have no big gaps in the design.
		Get 2 coins and masking tape. Put a piece of masking tape on each side of the coins. Write the words *Left* and *Right* on two sides of one coin and the words *Up* and *Down* on the other coin. With both coins in your hand, shake them and put the first one down, read what it says on the tape. If it says right, start in the top left corner and make your way to the right. Shake the other coin, and see whether it indicates to draw up or down. It may be easier if a friend or family member flips the coin so you can continue to draw. You can play this for as long as you wish.
		With standard grid paper, start in the top left corner and draw your way down to the bottom right, filling up as much of the paper as you can with the circuit board design. What did you notice?
		Draw an 8″ square on a blank piece of paper. Start drawing the design in the middle of the square and work around filling up the space.
		Draw an 8″ square on a blank piece of paper. Start drawing the design in the bottom left corner, draw your way to the opposite side, halfway up, and then finish up the design in the top left corner of the square.
		Fold a blank piece of paper in half. On one side, fill the paper with a very small-scale circuit board design; this can be a very effective filler. Then fill the second half of the paper with a large-scale circuit board design. What do you notice about how size can really change the effect of the design? How do you think you could use this design in your quilting?
		Get out the quilt sandwich. Draw your desired size on your sample and fill it for the next 5 minutes. Take a picture of this and share it with me. I totally want to see your progress and cheer you on.

TECHNICALLY SPEAKING
Computer Sleeve

Finished computer sleeve: 14½″ × 9½″

Making gifts for others adds a whole new level of thoughtfulness to your quilting—but making practical gifts takes your gift-giving to the next level. In this world full of technology, many of us have laptops that look very much the same, so it's fun to add your personality to your electronics by making a quilted computer sleeve. I wouldn't be surprised if you can't make just one—not a worry, as they are fast and fun projects to make and to give away.

MATERIALS AND SUPPLIES

Yardage is based on 44˝–wide fabric.

Fabric A: ½ yard for main fabric

Fabric B: ⅓ yard contrasting fabric for strips and binding

Fabric C: ½ yard for backing/lining

Batting: 18˝ × 38˝

Hair elastic: For button loop
(*Or use 3˝ length of elastic.*)

Button: ¾˝–2˝ diameter

CUTTING

Fabric A

· Cut 6 rectangles 4½˝ × 9½˝.

· Cut 6 squares 4½˝ × 4½˝.

· Cut 3 squares 2½˝ × 2½˝.

Fabric B

· Cut 3 rectangles 2½˝ × 9½˝.

· Cut 9 rectangles 2½˝ × 4½˝.

· Cut 2 strips 2½˝ × WOF for binding.

CONSTRUCTION

Seam allowances are ¼˝ unless otherwise noted. Press all the seams away from the center.

Block Assembly

Make 3 blocks.

1. Refer to the layout chart to piece the rectangles and squares as shown. With right sides together, stitch the 3 vertical columns. Press the seams outward on the outside columns and inward on the middle column.
▶ **FIG.A**

2. With right sides together, sew the columns from Step 1 together to complete the block. Repeat to create the other 2 blocks. Press the seams outward on 2 blocks and inward on 1 block.

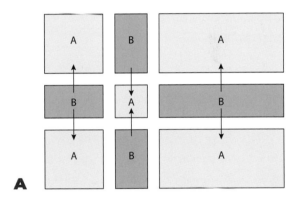

A

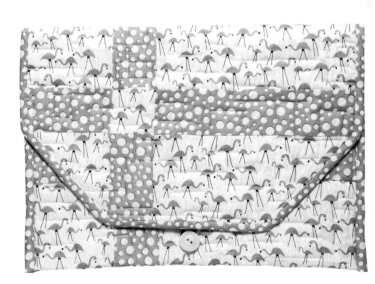

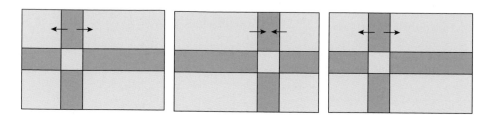

▶ DARA'S TIP *If you are using directional fabric, make 2 blocks with the contrast strip on the left and 1 block with the contrast strip on the right. Press the seams inward on the right-sided block and outward on the two left-sided blocks.*

3. To make one continuous panel, sew the 3 blocks together along the long edges so the contrast strips align and the seams nest. **▶ FIG.B**

▶ DARA'S TIP *This block can be used in multiple ways! When I showed it to my 16-year-old son, he thought it would make a great purse or even a large fanny pack. All you need to do is add straps to the back that could slide into belt loops. I can't wait to see what you do with this fun project.*

Free-Motion Quilting

1. Baste the computer cover to backing and batting with your preferred method (see Basting a Quilt, page 34).

2. Attach the darning foot.

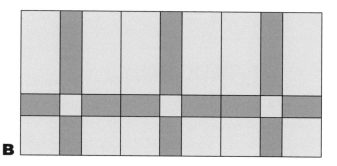

B

3. Free-motion quilt with a circuit board design or as desired. Circuit board quilting is fairly straightforward. I highly recommend that you go through the workouts to gain confidence. Before quilting, decide on the size and scale of your quilting to assure consistency.

4. Trim the quilted panel to 30½″ × 15½″.

Shaping and Making the Computer Cover

1. Shape the front flap at the top of the computer cover. At one short end of the quilted panel, measure 2˝ up the side and 2˝ toward the center on each side of the computer cover, and mark with pins or a fabric-marking pen. Line up the ruler against the 2˝ markings and draw cutting lines on each side. Cut along the marked lines. ▶ **FIGS.C–D**

2. Make the binding (see Making and Attaching Binding, page 37).

3. Cut a 17˝ length of binding and stitch it to the short end of the cover opposite the shaped front flap. Trim the extra binding. ▶ **FIG.E**

4. Fold the bottom third of the sleeve up so that the bound edge aligns with the start of the front flap and forms the opening for the computer. Baste ⅛˝ from the raw edges on both sides. Attach the binding to the sleeve from the back, sewing through both layers where you've basted the sides and one layer around the flap. Start at the bottom fold by wrapping 1˝ of the binding to the front side along the raw edge, as shown. Continue to attach the binding, sewing up one side, around the flap, and down the other side. ▶ **FIG.F**

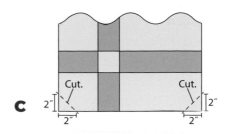

C Cut. 2˝ 2˝ Cut. 2˝ 2˝

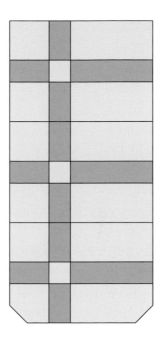

D

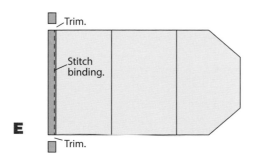

E Trim. Stitch binding. Trim.

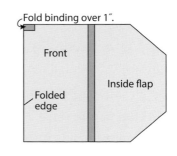

F Fold binding over 1˝. Front Inside flap Folded edge

▶ **DARA'S TIP** *The best way to attach the binding around the corners (of the front flap) is to put the needle down in the corner of the turn and pivot the fabric slightly and continue stitching. Sometimes it is helpful to make a small fold in the fabric to make the turn nice and clean.*

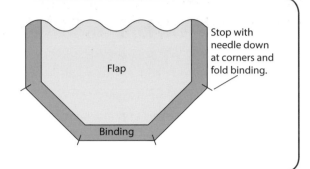

5. Once you reach the fold on the opposite side of the sleeve, cut away the binding leaving a 1″ tail. Fold the tail to the right side and stitch it down along the previously stitched seam. ▶ **FIG.G**

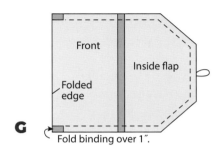

6. Press the binding flat all the way around and then over the seams. Stitch the binding in place around all the edges on the front side. You might want to catch an elastic or ribbon at the top of the flap (see Finishing, below) to help keep the sleeve closed. This helps create a nice crisp finish.

Finishing

1. There are a few ways to close the sleeve. I used a hair elastic with a button, but hook–and–loop tape, a snap, or even ribbon would work.

2. Sew the button to the center front of the case, 2″ from the bottom edge. Stitch the ends of the elastic or ribbon to the wrong side of the flap so the elastic slides around the button and holds the sleeve closed.

3. Slide the computer inside the case and do up the button for safe travels and safe keeping.

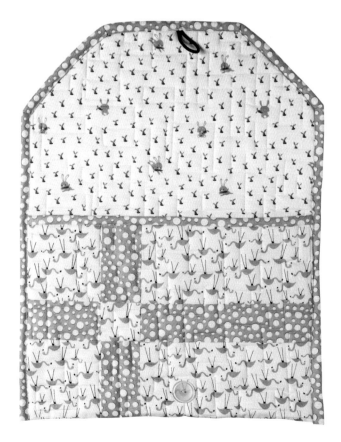

Finished quilt: 70˝ × 70˝ (5 rows across and 7 rows down)

Perhaps the recipient of the computer sleeve wants to snuggle under a coordinating quilt while typing. Here are brief instructions to make it happen.

MATERIALS AND SUPPLIES

Fabric A: 3¾ yards main fabric

Fabric B: 1⅝ yards strip fabric

Fabric C: 5 yards for binding and backing

Batting: 78˝ × 78˝

CUTTING

Fabric A

- Cut 18 strips 4½˝ × WOF.
  Subcut 70 rectangles 4½˝ × 8½˝.

- Cut 9 strips 4½˝ × WOF.
  Subcut 70 squares 4½˝ × 4½˝;
  then cut 3 squares 2½˝ × 2½˝.

- Cut 2 strips 2½˝ × WOF.
  Subcut 35 squares 2½˝ × 2½˝.

Fabric B

- Cut 9 strips 2½˝ × WOF.
  Subcut 35 strips 2½˝ × 8½˝
  and 10 strips 2½˝ × 4½˝.

- Cut 11 strips 2½˝ × WOF.
  Subcut 95 strips 2½˝ × 4½˝.

Fabric C

- Cut 2 rectangles 78˝ × WOF. Sew them together lengthwise for backing.

- Cut 8 strips 2½˝ × WOF for binding.

INSTRUCTIONS

Construct the blocks as for the computer sleeve. Make 17 blocks with the squares on the left; make 18 blocks with the squares on the right. Refer to the quilt photo to lay out the blocks, and then baste the quilt and FMQ!

CHAPTER 12

Quilting Wishbones and Fancy L's

Skills You Learn

WHAT YOU NEED

- Darning foot
- Quilt sandwich, 15˝ square

- How to use a darning foot
- Stitching on a quilt sandwich
- Moving the three layers of fabric under a needle with a darning foot
- Quilting a design along a prescribed line
- Spacing distance and height

DESIGN ELEMENTS: WISHBONES AND FANCY L'S

I only watched the television show *Laverne and Shirley* a few times when I was a kid, but that fancy L-shape that Laverne wore so prominently left a lasting impression on me.

When I saw this "wishbone" quilting design, I remembered that fancy L. Now when I stitch this out, I often imagine that I am creating rows of fancy L's.

1. Draw the starting line up in a curve or a hook. This line will be half the size of the main design. ▶ **FIG.A**

2. Curve the line down and out away from the hook, forming a loop. ▶ **FIG.B**

3. Draw a hook of equal size at the bottom and then curve the line upward and slanted toward the right to create the next hook. ▶ **FIG.C**

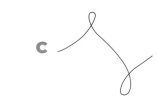

4. Repeat the same process to extend and travel the design. Keep spacing consistent and the size and shape of the hook the same. Remember that this design can be stretched into a variety of shapes and sizes. ▶ **FIG.D**

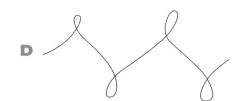

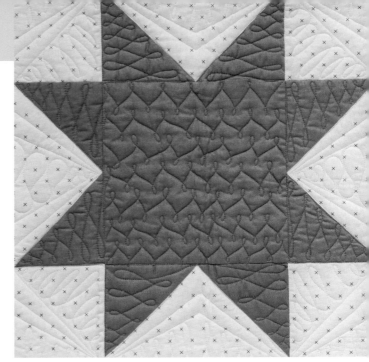

5. What do you notice about the design? The spacing is consistent between L's, the height is the same on the top and bottom, and the hooks or loops are similar in size. Although the space between designs, the height and the sizes of the loops can be changed, the key is to be consistent within a specific design. ▶ **FIG.E**

E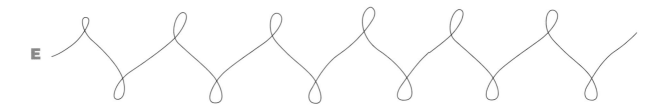

▶ **DARA'S TIP** *Keeping the flow of this linear design is important. Whenever possible, it is a good idea to use the piecing of the quilt as a guide as you FMQ. Before going to the sewing machine, practice on a lined piece of paper. Turn the paper lines facing up and down. Use the lines as a target to hit the centers of the design.*

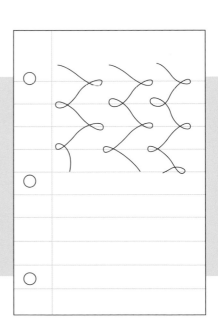

Design Variations

Just look at what you can do with these five wishbone design variations. Which one will you try first?

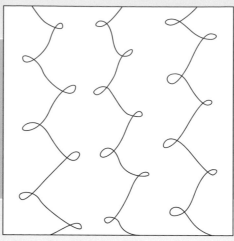

Descending Zag

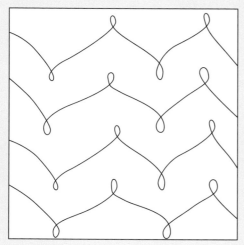

Chevron

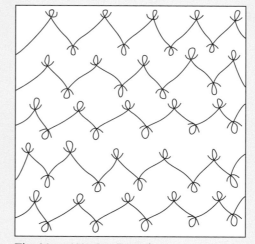

The More We Get Together

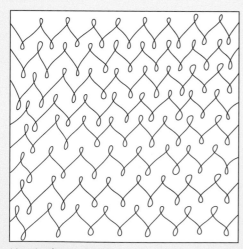

Herringbone Twist

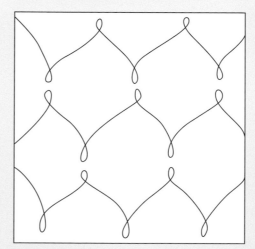

Spaced Out

Practice Workouts

Date	Time	Task
		With a lined piece of paper, using 2 lines, start on the left and make your way to the right drawing Continuous Lucky 8's. Keep going for 5 minutes, not ever lifting the pen.
		Put on the timer for 5 minutes and see how many lines you can draw.
		Turn the lined paper on its side so that the lines will provide you with guides in your spacing. Every time your Continuous Lucky 8 touches a line, curve it around until it hits the next line. Continue drawing until the timer goes off after 5 minutes.
		Elongate the Lucky 8's. With the lined paper going up and down, stretch out the design every fourth line. It should be no taller than 1˝ high. Set timer for 5 minutes.
		Experiment with the size of the loop on the top and bottom of the design. Set the timer at 5 minutes and see what you come up with.
		On a blank sheet of paper, draw 3 consecutive rows approximately 1˝ wide and leave 1˝ open between each line. In a different color pen, stagger the same design throughout the 3 rows, starting on the top row. What do you think of this secondary design?
		Draw a 4˝ square and play around with the design. How do you use the design to fill the space? Do you repeat the same design? Do you modify the size of one element of the design?
		Draw a 4˝ × 8˝ rectangle and fill the space. Try to do something different than what you have done so far.
		Draw an oval shape with a slight indent in the middle that is approximately 5˝ × 8˝. Fill the space. This is a good challenge because the design needs to stretch to fill the irregular shape.
		With the quilt sandwich, practice this new design by filling an eye-shape design, approximately 4˝ × 10˝.

CONTINUOUS FANCY EIGHTS
Builder Quilt

Finished quilt: 49˝ × 49˝

*I designed this quilt with the continuous–L (wishbone) design in mind.
By piecing same-size rows, it is easy to FMQ within the width of the rows.
You can change the quilt size to fit your needs.*

Quilt shown vertically

MATERIALS AND SUPPLIES

Yardage is based on 44″-wide fabric. When you select the fabric, pick 3 fabrics that are similar colors for the rectangles. Then select 6 coordinating fabrics to go with the first colors. These 6 fabrics are paired into 3 groups and each pair is assigned to one of the rectangle fabrics.

Fabrics A, B, and C: ½ yard each for rectangle blocks

Contrast fabrics (6): ⅓ yard of each for 3 sets of squares

Binding: ½ yard

Backing: 3¼ yards

Batting: 57″ × 57″

CUTTING

Fabric A

- Cut 4 strips 4″ × WOF.
  Subcut 18 rectangles 7½″ × 4″.

Fabric B

- Cut 3 strips 4″ × WOF.
  Subcut 14 rectangles 7½″ × 4″.

Fabric C

- Cut 4 strips 4″ × WOF.
  Subcut 18 rectangles 7½″ × 4″.

Contrast fabrics (square sets)

- From each of the 6 contrast fabrics, cut 2 strips 4″ × WOF. Pair 2 different fabrics together into a set of 4 strips; repeat for a total of 3 sets of 4 strips each.

Binding

- Cut 6 strips 2½″ × WOF.

Backing

- Cut 57″ × 57″, pieced as needed.

CONSTRUCTION

Seam allowances are ¼˝ unless otherwise noted.

Block and Quilt Assembly

1. For each square set, take 1 pair of contrast fabric strips and sew them together lengthwise with right sides together into strip sets. You'll have 2 strip sets for each pair of fabrics. Press the seam allowances to the darker fabric and subcut each strip set into 4˝ square units. You should get 10 units from each strip set. This produces more units than required, but you can use them to fill in gaps. We'll call these square sets 1, 2, and 3.

A

2. Keeping the square units in the same order and with right sides together, sew square set units to rectangles as follows:

a. Sew square set 1 units to the bottom edge of the rectangles cut from fabric A.

b. Sew square set 2 units to the bottom edge of the rectangles cut from fabric B.

c. Sew square set 3 units to the bottom edge of the rectangles cut from fabric C. ▶ **FIG.A**

3. Square up these blocks to 7½˝ × 7½˝.

4. Refer to the quilt assembly diagram for the sequence of the columns. Please note:

· *Block A:* Fabric A + square set 1
Block B: Fabric B + square set 2
Block C: Fabric C + square set 3

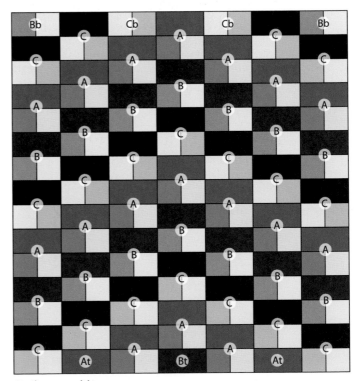

Quilt assembly

- *Columns 1, 3, 5, and 7:* These columns are made up of whole blocks A, B, and C with a square set at the top:

  Columns 1 and 7: **Bb** = bottom half of Block B

  Columns 3 and 5: **CB** = bottom half of Block C.

- *Columns 2, 4, and 6:* The bottom of each column has a rectangle instead of a whole block:

  Column 2: **At** = Top rectangle of Block A

  Column 4: **Bt** = Top rectangle of Block B

Column 6: **At** = Top rectangle of Block A

Piece the columns one at a time. Press the seams of columns 1, 3, 5, and 7 facing down and the seams of columns 2, 4, and 6 facing up. This helps "nest" the seams.

Free-Motion Quilting

1. Baste the quilt to the backing and batting using your preferred method (see Basting a Quilt, page 34).

2. Attach the darning foot.

3. The direction you want the eye to travel determines the directionality of the quilting. The quilt has a "Bargello" effect as the main colors create a V-shape. If you want to accentuate the movement in piecing, follow the main colors with the stitching. I recommend stitching across the quilt in the already existing rows. I purposely created the quilt with 4˝ strips so that this wishbone style quilting fits easily. Using the piecing of the quilt as guidelines for quilting is genius—you're welcome! ▶ **FIG.B**

Finishing

1. Trim the quilt so the edges are even.

2. Make and attach the binding (see Making and Attaching Binding, page 37).

3. Feel free to attach your own special label (see Quilt Labels, page 39).

4. Prepare for warm snuggles.

B

CHAPTER 13

Quilting Ribbon Candy

WHAT YOU NEED

- Darning foot
- Quilt or quilt sand–wich, 15˝ square
- Right angle square quilting ruler
- Marking pen

Skills You Learn

- How to use a darning foot
- Stitching on a quilt sandwich
- Moving the three layers of fabric under a needle with a darning foot
- Spacing distance and height
- Mirroring a design
- Creating a design within a design
- Quilting a design along a prescribed line

DESIGN ELEMENT: RIBBON CANDY CURVES

To create a successful ribbon candy design, the curves and spacing need to be consistent. This design works best when travelling along a line within a specific space or area. Although the ribbon candy design can be stitched to fit in many different shape and size areas, the curves and spacing of the design itself need to be uniform. I would not quilt this design in spaces that are larger than 2½˝ because larger areas make it more difficult to ensure that the design is uniform and consistent.

1. The very beginning of the stitching is where the shape, the size (scale), and the spacing are established. Consistency is very important, so this first step is to create the angle of the curve as it dips in. ▶ **FIG.A**

2. Focus next on the drawing the same curve at the top only outward instead of inward. Notice how the curves are almost identical, just flipped. I find that similar curves produce a beautiful flow to the design. ▶ **FIG.B**

3. Now that the ribbon candy design has two matching curves, the "bumps" of the design can continue on. Remember to focus on making the curves the same coming into the curve and then coming out of the curve. ▶ **FIG.C**

4. See the quilting progression of this design. Trace it with your finger. ▶ **FIG.D**

5. After a bit of practice, try creating different size designs, just make sure to create the same curve when it is time to bend into the design. To really grasp how to change the scale of these designs, try tracing these variations with your finger so you can feel the similar curves in each sequence regardless of the height and depth of the design. ▶ **FIGS.E–J**

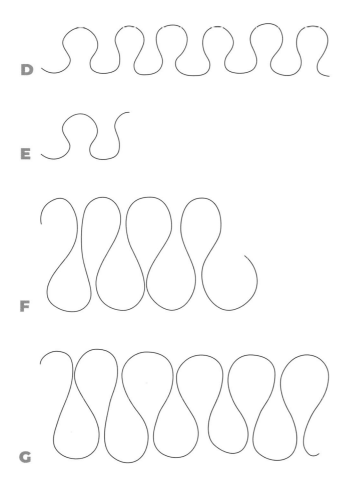

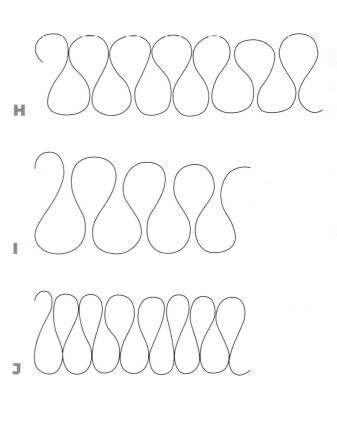

Design Variations

Here are five variations of the ribbon candy design. Which one will you try first?

Hearts

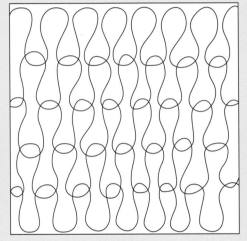

Round and Round We Go

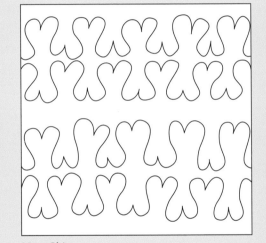

Hop Skip

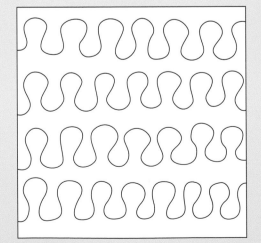

Octopus

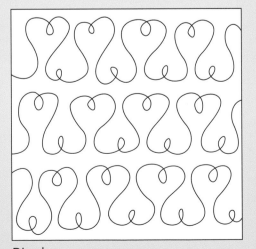

Dimple

Practice Workouts

Date	Time	Task
		With a lined piece of paper, start at the left side and work your way to the right on a single line, staying within the lines and create the ribbon candy design. Do not lift your pen. Try not to cross lines. Draw for 5 minutes.
		Do the same exercise as in first workout, but use two lines to draw the design, so the design is twice as big. Continue for 5 minutes.
		On lined piece of paper, using two lines as a guide for height, draw the ribbon candy and cross at the top and bottom of each bend.
		On a lined piece of paper, draw ribbon candy as if it has been stretched out; experiment with this for 5 minutes.
		On blank piece of paper, draw an 8″ square. Then draw a 10″ square around it so it has a 2″ border. In that border, draw ribbon candy all the way around.
		Fill the inside of the square as you wish with the ribbon candy design. Will you draw large or small? Will you draw left to right? Will you draw bottom to top?
		On a lined piece of paper, draw a line of the ribbon candy, but instead of nicely rounded bottoms and tops, indent them. What do you see? Draw for 5 minutes.
		On a blank piece of paper, draw a large eye shape about 10″ × 5″. Starting from the left to the right, fill the space with the ribbon candy design.
		Draw a large square about 8″ and draw a line from the top left to the bottom right. Fill both sides of the square with ribbon candy.
		Get out a quilt sandwich. Stitch a rectangle 4″ × 10″. Divide it in half on the diagonal. Fill in both sides.

X'S AND O'S
Quilt

Finished quilt: 75½″ × 88″
Finished blocks: 12½″ × 12½″

One of the main reasons I quilt is to show love to those around me. A quilt is soft and warm. It provides comfort and love. This quilt design was inspired by X's and O's—meaning the recipient has lots of hugs and kisses from the maker and giver of the quilt.

Quilt shown horizontally

MATERIALS AND SUPPLIES

Yardage is based on 44˝-wide fabric.

There are 7 rows in this quilt, each row has 6 blocks, and each block is made with 3 fabrics. Color A is white (or other background color or print) and is used in every row, color B is the lighter shade, and color C is the darker shade. The 6 blocks in each row feature 2 variations, which are referred to as X blocks and O blocks.

Fabric A (white): 3½ yards for background

Fabric B (7 light colors): ⅔ yard of each: light red, light pink, light peach, light cream, light green, light blue, and light purple

Fabric C (7 dark colors): ½ yard of each: dark red, dark pink, dark peach, yellow, dark green, dark blue, and dark purple

Binding: ¾ yard

Backing: 5½ yards

Batting: 84˝ × 96˝

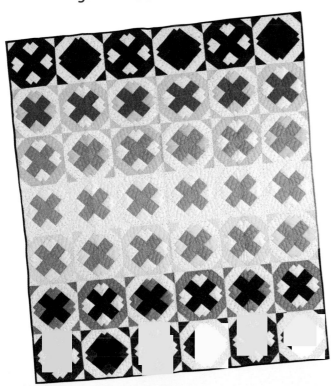

CUTTING

Fabric A (white)

- Cut 28 strips 3˝ × WOF

- Cut 8 strips 2½˝ × WOF.
  Subcut into 84 rectangles 2½˝ × 3½˝

- Cut 4 strips 2½˝ × WOF.
  Subcut into 8 strips 2½˝ × 20˝.

- Cut 4 strips 1½˝ × WOF.
  Subcut into 8 strips 1½˝ × 20˝.

Fabric B (light colors)

From each of the 6 light colors:

- Cut 1 strip 3½˝ × WOF.
  Subcut into 12 rectangles 3½˝ × 2½˝.

- Cut 4 strips 3˝ × WOF.

- Cut 1 strip 1½˝ × WOF.
  Subcut into 2 strips 1½˝ × 20˝.

Fabric C (dark colors)

- From each of the 6 dark colors,
  cut 3 strips 3½˝ × WOF.
  Subcut into 30 squares 3½˝ × 3½˝.

Binding

- Cut 9 strips 2½˝ × WOF.

Backing

- Piece vertically to make
  1 rectangle 84˝ × 96˝.

Pieced by
Moira Porter

CONSTRUCTION

Seam allowances are ¼˝ unless otherwise noted.

X-Block Assembly

The following instructions are for each color set (rows 1–7). Make 3 X blocks for each row. ▶ **FIG.A**

1. Sew fabric A 1½˝ × 20˝ to fabric B 2½˝ × 20˝ and press toward the darker color.

2. Subcut into 12 rectangles 1½˝ × 3½˝. ▶ **FIG.B**

3. Stitch a unit from Step 2 to a fabric B (2½˝ × 3½˝) rectangle and press. Trim to 3½˝ × 3½˝. ▶ **FIG.C**

4. Lay out the fabric C squares and the squares made in Step 3 in the order as shown. Pay attention to the direction of the units so that the corners are in the appropriate spots. Press seams as shown. These are called Nine-Patch blocks. ▶ **FIG.D**

5. To make the triangle corners sew 4 strips sets by attaching the 3˝-wide strips of fabric A to the 3˝-wide strips of fabric B for each light color. Press the seams to the darker side. ▶ **FIG.E**

6. Use a right angle ruler to cut the triangles. On each strip set, make a mark 11½˝ from one end along the bottom of the strip and cut a triangle 5½˝ high. Then flip your ruler and cut a triangle from the top of the strip. Keep flipping the ruler—you will be able to cut 6 triangles out of each strip set.

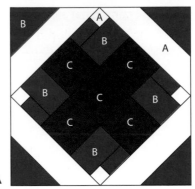

A

X block

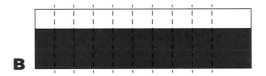

B

C

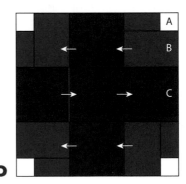

D

E

The mostly white triangles are for the X block and the mostly colored triangles are for the O block. ▶ FIG.F

F

7. Mark the center of one side of a Nine-Patch block and the center of the long edge of a mostly white triangle. Pin and stitch the pieces; the triangle piece will extend beyond the edge of the slightly on both sides—this is necessary for attaching the other side triangles. Add three more triangles around the remaining sides of the Nine-Patch block. Trim the block to 13˝ × 13˝. ▶ FIG.G

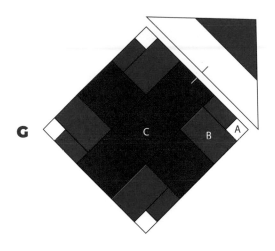

G

O-Block Assembly

1. The process for making the O blocks is the same as that for making the X blocks, with differences in color placement. Keep in mind you have already prepped some parts of the O block (see X-Block Assembly, Step 6, previous page), so these blocks will come together quickly. ▶ FIG.H

2. Attach the 1½˝ × 20˝ fabric B strip to the 2½˝ × 20˝ fabric A strip (see X-Block Assembly, Steps 1–3, previous page). Press the seams to the dark side. Subcut into 12 units 1½˝ × 3½˝.

3. Stitch a unit from Step 2 to a fabric A (2½˝ × 3½˝) rectangle and press. Trim to 3½˝ × 3½˝.

4. Lay out the blocks in the order as shown. Pay attention to the direction of the blocks so that the corners are in the appropriate spots. Use the fabric C squares and the units from the previous step to make the

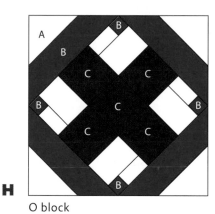

H

O block

Nine-Patch blocks. Press the seams as for the X blocks.

5. Using the previously made O triangles, attach the first triangle to the top right side of the block, remembering to find the centers and attach them with overages on either side. Then attach the bottom left triangle and finally the triangles on either side. Trim the block to 13˝ × 13˝.

Preparing the Quilt Front

1. Lay out the blocks as shown. ▶ FIG.I

2. With right sides together, sew the blocks to create the rows. Press all the even rows to the right and all the odd rows to the left. Pressing this way will allow the seams to nest.

3. After all the blocks are sewn into rows, stitch the rows with right sides together. Feel free to follow the color order of the rows shown in the photo, but you can also change the order as desired.

X	O	X	O	X	O
O	X	O	X	O	X
X	O	X	O	X	O
O	X	O	X	O	X
X	O	X	O	X	O
O	X	O	X	O	X
X	O	X	O	X	O

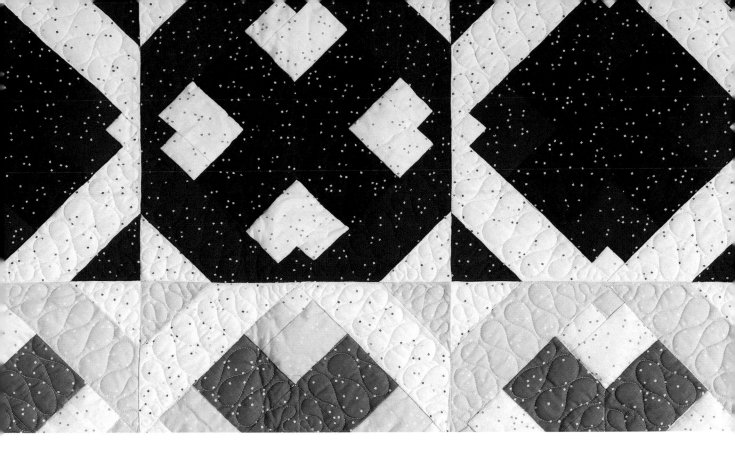

Free-Motion Quilting

1. Baste the quilt to the backing and batting with your preferred method (See Basting a Quilt, page 34).

2. Attach the darning foot.

3. Free-motion quilt using the spacing of the blocks to help form consistently sized and shaped ribbon candy designs.

Finishing

1. Trim the quilt so the edges are even.

2. Prepare and attach the binding (see Making and Attaching Binding, page 37).

CHAPTER 14

Quilting Clamshells

Skills You Learn

- How to use a darning foot
- Stitching on a quilt sandwich
- Moving the three layers of fabric under a needle with a darning foot
- Quilting a design along a prescribed line
- Spacing distance and height
- Creating a design within a design
- Mirroring a design

WHAT YOU NEED

- Darning foot
- Quilt sandwich, 15˝ square

DESIGN ELEMENT: CLAMSHELLS

There is incredible diversity within the clamshell design. I love how an arch can be transformed in so many ways with the establishment of good visual spacing along a baseline. Start this design by turning a lined piece of paper sideways so you can use the lines as jump off points to help establish the muscle memory of proper spacing. Getting the right spacing as a foundation to build on is critical in establishing great design. At the beginning of my quilting I use a marking pen and a ruler to mark my lines to make sure I had proper spacing.

Once the foundation of the clamshell has been established, the design needs to be staggered when travelling back for the second row, similar to how brick is laid. So, creating a half-design at the beginning and ending of alternating rows is necessary.

1. Creating nice curved arches is a skill that requires practice. Using paper or a quilt with a grid to help create this muscle memory is a great way to start. You can also use plastic grid rulers to mark the design on fabric. ▶ **FIG.A**

2. To build a second row, the beginning of the clamshell needs to "touch" the center of a clamshell from the previous row, as shown. I liken this to a little frog or bunny that is hopping along all the centers of the previous row. If you feel that the clams are not centered, use a clear ruler to check your accuracy. If there is need for more accuracy, draw lines with chalk or an erasable marker to establish better lines. ▶ **FIG.B**

3. Create smaller shapes for better accuracy. I recommend keeping the clams under 2˝. ▶ **FIG.C**

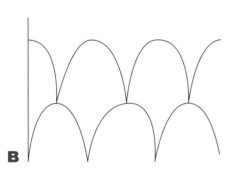

B

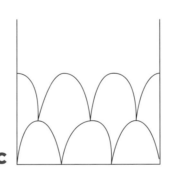

C

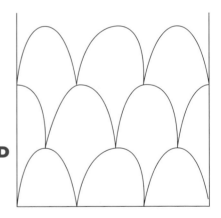

D

4. If this is a difficult design to grasp at first, do not despair—practice really helps. Practice by doodling on paper. Try practicing with grid paper. Make the design slightly smaller so you feel like you have more control. But most importantly, do not stop trying. ▶ **FIG.D**

5. Add as many rows as you would like, this design just gets better and better. ▶ **FIG.E**

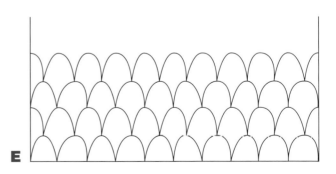

E

Design Variations

Just look at what you can do with these five clamshell design variations. Which one will you try first?

Triple Play

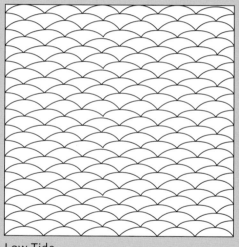

Low Tide

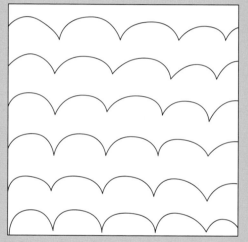

Echo

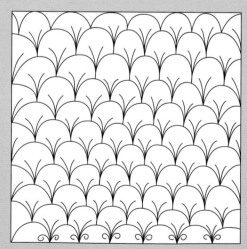

Fancy Pants

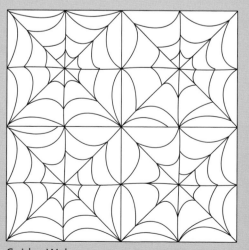

Spider Web

Practice Workouts

Date	Time	Task
		Use standard grid paper to create 3 rows of clams. Each clam will be 4 lines wide and 4 lines high. Remember when adding a row on top of the baseline to hit the centers.
		Practice drawing small clams. Draw clams 2 spaces or units apart. Draw for 5 minutes.
		Practice drawing large clams. Draw them 8 spaces wide and 5 spaces high. Set the timer for 5 minutes.
		Practice changing the size of the clams from large to small, alternating rows for 5 minutes.
		Draw skinny clams. Make them 2 spaces wide but 6 spaces high for 5 minutes.
		Draw more skinny clams, but this time double up the clams in each row. Draw for 5 minutes.
		Draw clams 4 spaces wide and 4 spaces high. Fill the inside of each clam with a loop.
		Get out a quilt sandwich. Fill a 5″ square with medium-size rows of clams.
		In another 5″ square, create rows of clams that are alternate sizes. For example, stitch medium-size clams in the first row, shallow-size clams in the second row, and large-size clams in the third row; continue to fill the square.
		Make an 8″ × 6″ rectangle on the quilt sandwich. Create a clam wall with each row averaging 1″ wide. Use your imagination to fill in the spaces differently on each row. See the designs shared in this chapter for inspiration.

CHECKERBOARD
Quilt Set

Finished quilt: 19½″ × 25½″

This project was designed with clamshells in mind because the squares provide a great framework for quilting.

MATERIALS AND SUPPLIES

Yardage is based on 44˝–wide fabric.

Fabric A (dark color): ¾ yard
for checkerboard squares and binding

Fabric B (light color): ⅓ yard
for checkerboard squares

Fabric C (coordinating color): ½ yard
for outer border and pockets

Backing: ⅞ yard

Batting: 26˝ × 32˝

Hook–and–loop tape: 8˝ × 1˝
(such as Velcro)

Ribbon: ¾ yard

CUTTING

Fabric A

· Cut 4 strips 2½˝ × WOF.

· Cut 3 strips 2½˝ × WOF for binding.

Fabric B

· Cut 2 strips 2½˝ × WOF.

Fabric C

· Cut 1 strip 2˝ × WOF.
  Subcut into 2 strips 2˝ × 16½˝.

· Cut 1 strip 5˝ × WOF.
  Subcut into 2 strips 5˝ × 19½˝.

· Cut 1 strip 4˝ × WOF. Subcut into
  4 rectangles 4˝ × 8˝ for pockets.

CONSTRUCTION

*Seam allowances are ¼˝ unless
otherwise noted.*

Piecing the Checkerboard

1. Create one large strip set by sewing
fabric A–B–A–B–A–B–A together (save
the remaining strip for later). Press the
seams toward the darker fabric. Cut the
strip in half lengthwise. Refer to each
section as part 1 and 2. ▶ **FIG.A**

2. Cut the remaining strip B in
half lengthwise.

3. Sew one half of strip B to
the top edge of part 1. Sew the
remaining half of strip B to the
bottom edge of part 2. Press
the newly sewn strip sets.

	Part 1		Cut.	Part 2	
A					
B					
A					
B					
A					
B					
A					

A

4. Subcut part 1 and part 2 into 2½˝ × 16½˝ strips, cutting 4 strips each. (You will have enough of parts 1 and 2 to make a second checkerboard if you want.) ▶ **FIG.B**

5. Sew all 8 newly cut strips together in true checkerboard fashion, alternating rows. ▶ **FIG.C**

6. The pieced checkerboard should measure 16½˝ × 16½˝.

7. With right sides together, sew the 2 side borders (2˝ × 16½˝) to the checkerboard. Press the seams facing outward.

8. With right sides together, sew the 2 end borders (5˝ × 19½˝) to the top and bottom of the checkerboard. Press the seams facing outward.

Making the Pockets

Make two pockets to hold the checkerboard markers. In my case, I plan to use buttons from my extensive button collection as checkers! You can also use felt circles, rocks, shells, or even coins!

1. Cut the hook–and–loop tape in half. Pin the soft (loop) side of one of the strips to the right side of one 4˝ × 8˝ pocket piece, centered and 2˝ down from the top edge. Stitch the hook–and–loop tape in place. Repeat on a second pocket piece. ▶ **FIG.D**

2. Save the hook pieces of the hook–and–loop tape to put on the checkerboard top once the finished pockets are pinned in place.

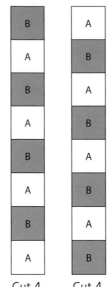

B

Cut 4. Cut 4.

C

D

2˝

Hook-and-loop tape

Pocket
right side

3. Pin 2 pocket rectangles, one with hook-and-loop tape and one without hook-and-loop tape, with right sides together and sew from the bottom right all the way around the edge to the bottom left corner. Repeat with remaining 2 pocket pieces. Trim the corners, turn the pockets right side out, and press. These will be attached after the free-motion quilting is finished.

Free-Motion Quilting

1. Baste the checkerboard to the backing and batting with your preferred method (see Basting a Quilt, page 34).

2. Attach the darning foot.

3. Having completed the 10 clamshell design workouts, you will have mastered a variety of designs. Choose one clamshell design, and with the quilting diagram for reference, it's time to free-motion quilt. I encourage you to make this your very own by putting your own twist on it.

▶ **FIG.E**

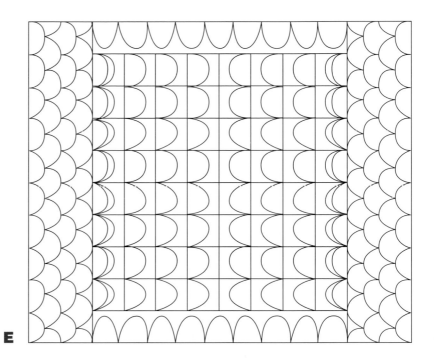

E

Finishing

1. After quilting, square up the checkerboard.

2. Position the two pockets on the opposite ends and sides of the checkerboard, 1˝ from the side edge and with the unsewn edge of the pocket aligned with the top or bottom edge of the border. Make sure the loop half of the hook-and-loop tape is facing down so you can pin mark the location for the hook half on the border fabric.

3. Set the pockets aside, and stitch the hook-and-loop tape (hook) pieces at the markings so they will align with the loop pieces.

4. Reposition the pockets and make sure the hook-and-loop tape strips line up. Stitch the sides of the pockets to the quilt.

5. Fold the ribbon in half. Pin the center of the folded ribbon to the center of one of the wider borders so the ends of the ribbon are over the checkerboard; baste the fold of the ribbon in place.

6. Make and attach the binding to the checkerboard, catching the bottom of the pockets and the ribbon in the binding (see Making and Attaching Binding, page 37). ▶ **FIG.F**

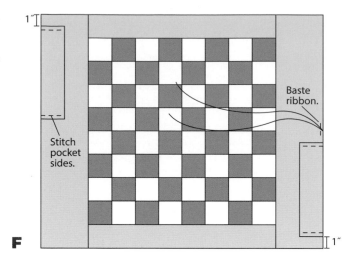

1″

Baste ribbon.

Stitch pocket sides.

1″

F

▶ **DARA'S TIP** *It is always a lot of fun to add embellishments to projects. I absolutely love the orange glasses on the dog featured on the print in this checkerboard, so I thought it would be awesome to add orange piping on the top edge of the pockets. Just think of the ways you can add your own special touches to your projects.*

APPENDIX

Sawtooth Star Block

The Sawtooth Star block that you see featured in each of the project chapters is easy to make and then transform into the perfect quilt sampler to showcase all you learned about free-motion quilting. Use all ten design elements to free-motion a quilt of any size!

Having the background and border use the same fabric allows the quilting designs to stand out. And it's fun to use straight lines to create some new quilting spaces. The sample quilt was made with 12″ blocks, but the chart below gives cutting instructions for several different sizes.

Sawtooth Star Sampler, 42″ × 57″, by Dara Tomasson, pieced by Becky Keizer

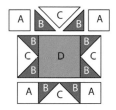
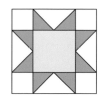

For	Cut	Subcut	Block size					
			4″	**6″**	**8″**	**10″**	**12″**	**15″**
A	4 squares		1½″	2″	2½″	3″	3½″	4¼″
B	4 squares	8 triangles*	1⅞″	2⅜″	2⅞″	3⅜″	3⅞″	4⅝″
C	1 square	4 triangles**	3¼″	4¼″	5¼″	6¼″	7¼″	8¾″
D	1 square		2½″	3½″	4½″	5½″	6½″	8″

* For 8 triangles, subcut 4 squares diagonally once.

** For 4 triangles, subcut 1 square diagonally twice.

RESOURCES

Project Specifics

Page 46: On a Roll Pencil Holder
Page 49: *Extra!* Straight-Line Stitched Quilt

Fabric (for pencil holder): Offshore 2 collection by Deena Rutter and Confetti Cotton Marmalade—for Riley Blake Designs

Fabric (for quilt): Offshore 2 collection by Deena Rutter and Confetti Cotton solids—for Riley Blake Designs

Elastic: 2″ Waistband Elastic from Riley Blake Designs

Batting: Hobbs Tuscany Collection 80% Cotton/20% Wool

Thread: Superior So Fine! #469 and #401

Page 54: Tote-ally Terrific Tote Bag

Fabric: Variety by Deena Rutter and Confetti Cotton solids—for Riley Blake Designs

Batting: Hobbs Tuscany Collection 80% Cotton/20% Wool and Hobbs Tuscany Collection 100% Wool

Thread: Superior So Fine! #401

Page 64: Heart of the Home Pillow Cover
Page 68: *Extra!* Log Cabin Quilt

Fabric: Hedge Rose collection by Kelly Panacci from Penny Rose Fabrics, Blossom collection by Christopher Thompson, and Confetti Cotton solids—for Riley Blake Designs

Batting: Hobbs Tuscany Collection Silk

Thread: Superior So Fine! #401

Page 74: He Loves Me, He Loves Me Not Apron
Page 81: *Extra!* Quick and Yummy Quilt

Fabric (for apron): Fox Farm collection by Melissa Mortenson of Polka Dot Chair and Confetti Cotton Riley Red—for Riley Blake Designs

Fabric (for quilt): Fox Farm collection by Melissa Mortenson of Polka Dot Chair, with Confetti Cotton Riley Red and Riley Navy (as backing)—for Riley Blake Designs

Rickrack: ¾″ crimson Sew Together by Riley Blake Designs

Batting: Hobbs Tuscany Collection 80% Cotton/20% Wool and Hobbs Tuscany Collection 100% Wool

Thread: Superior So Fine! #507 and #412

Page 86: Ohio Star Table Runner
Page 90: *Extra!* Ohio Star Quilt

Fabric: Farm Girl Vintage collection by Lori Holt of Bee in my Bonnet and Confetti Cotton solids—for Riley Blake Designs

Batting: Hobbs Tuscany Collection Silk and Hobbs Tuscany Collection 100% Wool

Thread: Superior So Fine! #401

Page 96: So Happy Together Place Mats
Page 101: *Extra!* Extra-Fun Place Mats

Fabric (for place mats): Gretel collection by Amy Smart from Penny Rose Fabrics—for Riley Blake Designs

Fabric (for extra-fun place mats): Felt letters with Someday collection by Minki Kim—for Riley Blake Designs

Batting: Hobbs Tuscany Collection Cotton Wool Blend

Thread: Superior So Fine! #401

Page 106: Technically Speaking Computer Sleeve
Page 111: *Extra!* Technically Speaking Quilt

Fabric: Gnome and Gardens collection by Shawn Wallace and Confetti Cotton solids—for Riley Blake Designs

Batting: Hobbs Tuscany Collection 100% Unbleached Cotton

Thread: Superior So Fine! #401

Page 116: Continuous Fancy Eights Builder Quilt

Fabric: Sweet Stems collection by Sue Daley Designs with Gabrielle Neil from Penny Rose Fabrics and Confetti Cotton solids—for Riley Blake Designs

Batting: Hobbs Heirloom Natural 100% Cotton

Thread: Superior So Fine! #521

Page 124: X's and O's Quilt

Fabric: Blossom collection by Christopher Thompson—for Riley Blake Designs

Batting: Hobbs Tuscany Collection 100% Wool and Hobbs Tuscany Collection 100% Unbleached Cotton

Thread: Superior So Fine! #433, #510, #469, #495, #517, #412, #401, #524

Page 134: Checkerboard Quilt Set

Fabric: Hey Mister collection by My Mind's Eye, Someday collection by Minki Kim, and Confetti Cotton Pumpkin—for Riley Blake Designs

Batting: Hobbs Tuscany Collection 100% Premium Polyester

Thread: Superior So Fine! #401

Additional Resources

Brother domestic sewing machines
I used the Nouvelle 1500 (no longer available on the Brother website; check for updated models). ▶ brother-usa.com

Gammill longarm machines
I used a version of the Statler that allows for hand-guided as well as computerized quilting (check the website for current models). ▶ gammill.com/products

Hobbs Batting ▶ hobbsbatting.com

Machingers Quilting Gloves—*for free-motion quilting* ▶ quilterstouch.com

Riley Blake Designs ▶ rileyblakedesigns.com

Superior Threads ▶ superiorthreads.com

Photo by Vanessa Lust Photography

ABOUT THE AUTHOR

DARA TOMASSON was born the third of six kids and discovered early the advantages of being independent. Learning to sew meant that she could make whatever she wanted—liberation! From sewing her own pair of shorts at age ten to countless dresses, skirts and pajama pants, her sewing efforts evolved to quilting at age nineteen, and she has not stopped since.

Dara recently moved from the Canadian prairies to Canada's tropics, Vancouver Island, where she happily uses all the time she used to spend shoveling snow for quilting. Dara, an aspiring coach, has the perfect number of children (five!) to form her very own basketball team, with her husband as spare. Coaching others, be it basketball or free-motion quilting, brings her so much joy. Dara has translated her professional teaching career of almost ten years in the public school system into a methodical, practical, and uplifting method of teaching free-motion quilting skills.

Dara accidentally became a quilter for hire when she started teaching quilting at her local quilt shop. When her students finished their quilts using her designs, Dara used her special skills to complete their samples with her signature style. After using boxes of spray baste and spending many hours on her hands and knees basting, Dara finally took the plunge and invested in a Gammill longarm machine. For the past four years, fellow Canadians and neighbors to the south have sent their quilts to Dara either in person or by mail so she could put her finishing touches on their beloved quilts.

When she isn't quilting, teaching quilting, or cheering her kids at their basketball games, Dara loves to collaborate with fabric companies, such as Riley Blake Designs and RJR Fabrics. Dara also publishes designs in collaboration books, makes videos on her YouTube channel, coordinates with local charity quilting efforts, and maintains an online and social media presence to share her creative pursuits. Dara is also a business and life coach for fellow quilters and creatives.

Visit Dara online and follow on social media!

▶ **Website:** daratomasson.com

▶ **Facebook:** /dara.bowietomasson

▶ **Instagram:** #daratomasson

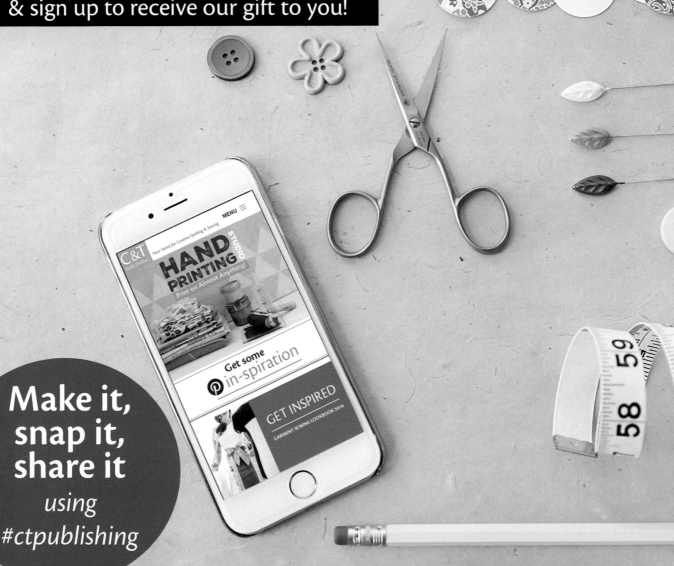